100 YEARS OF GREATNESS
COACH
JOHN WOODEN

Matt Fulks

TRIUMPH
BOOKS

Wooden stands amid his Bruins during the last timeout against Notre Dame in South Bend, Indiana on January 19, 1974. With 21 seconds remaining UCLA had the ball but was unable to score, ending their 88-game winning streak.

Triumph Books and colophon are registered
trademarks of Random House, Inc.

This book is available in quantity at special discounts for your group
or organization. For further information, contact:

Triumph Books
542 South Dearborn Street
Suite 750
Chicago, Illinois 60605
(312) 939-3330
Fax (312) 663-3557
www.triumphbooks.com

ISBN: 978-1-57243-937-5
Printed in United States of America

Content packaged by Mojo Media, Inc.
Joe Funk: Editor
Jason Hinman: Creative Director

All photographs courtesy of AP Images except where otherwise noted.

About the Author

Matt Fulks, who started his journalism career while attending Lipscomb University in Nashville, Tennessee, spends his time as a freelance writer, editor, "Mr. Mom," and co-host of a daily on-line radio show, "Behind the Stats," on SportsRadioKC.com. He is a regular contributor to various publications, including KCMetroSports.com and the Royals' Gameday magazine. He is the author/co-author of more than 15 books. Matt resides in the Kansas City area with his wife, Libby, and their three children. For more information visit www.MattFulks.com.

Contents

Wooden holds the NCAA championship trophy, which the Bruins won for the fifth straight year on March 27, 1971 by defeating Villanova University 68-62 in Houston, Texas.

Introduction

This book is a tribute to not only one of the best coaches of all-time in any sport, but also to one of the most humble individuals I've ever met.

My initial conversation with John Wooden was in 1994, while working on my first book, "Behind the Stats: Tennessee's Coaching Legends." At least three of the basketball coaches in that book studied and knew, to some extent, Wooden and his teachings. One of them, Don Meyer, who won the 2009 ESPN Jim Valvano ESPY Award, passed along Wooden's phone number for the interview.

I will never forget phoning him. I was 24, one year out of school but five years in this media racket, thinking that every interview would be a breeze. Yet, as I prepared to call Wooden, nervousness set in. The anticipation and butterflies as I pushed the buttons that first time were as bad as they were any time I called a pretty girl.

As the phone rang, a part of me hoped—almost prayed—that Wooden wouldn't answer. It'd be much easier to leave a message. Oh, good, I thought, as the answering machine began to tell me I was safe. That relief didn't last. Coach picked up during my message. But something odd happened. Almost immediately, my nerves were eased by this calming, gentle man on the other end.

By the end of that initial conversation, I realized—thanks in part to Wooden telling me so—that he'd be willing to talk any time I called. During the next 15 years, I did so as much as I could justify, for everything from articles and columns, to book projects and radio interviews. Each time was equally as thrilling for me.

In fact, one of my greatest professional thrills centers around John Wooden.

During the late 1990s, I was working on a book for CBS Sports titled "Stories from the Final Four." Coach Wooden agreed not only to be featured prominently in the book, but also allowed me to ghostwrite his stories. I was floored. My fourth book, and I was ghostwriting for John Wooden! Granted, there likely are dozens of writers who can say something similar, but to a 20-something kid from Kansas, that was a special moment.

Ultimately for me, the reason for writing this book—and something I hope you take away from it—might be best summed up in the words of Duke basketball coach Mike Krzyzewski: "Many have called Coach Wooden the 'gold standard' of coaches. I believe he was the 'gold standard' of people."

—Matt Fulks • June 2010

Wooden, who had announced he would retire from coaching after UCLA's NCAA championship game the following night, listens to comments during a news conference in San Diego on March 30, 1975.

Wooden holds the 32nd NCAA Men's Basketball championship trophy he received as the Bruins won their sixth NCAA basketball title after defeating Jacksonville 80-69 at College Park, Maryland on March 21, 1970.

The Passing of a Legacy

There really isn't an easy way to describe John Wooden. During August 1972, the summer after the UCLA Bruins won their sixth national championship in a row, the late Jim Murray, a *Los Angeles Times* sports columnist who was as revered in sports writing circles as Wooden was in basketball, came as close as anyone to portraying Wooden in words. Murray penned the following:

"He looks like the kind of guy you could get to guess which walnut has the pea under it. The eyes are a kind of a guileless blue, and the conversation is sprinkled with 'Oh, my goodness!' and 'Gracious!' and you bet he could never figure out how they sawed the lady in half, or got the rabbit into the hat. They run carnivals for guys like this, you feel sure."

Later in the column Murray added: "It is a conceit of our times that kids are supposed to be manageable only by their peer groups, that they are in headlong rebellion from any other authority and, the postulate has it, there is no way a street kid from Philadelphia or a blacktop player from Lexington Avenue could relate to a Bible reader from Indiana who coaches by wall motto. In a time when training table mutinies are as commonplace as any other forms of campus unrest, Wooden has managed to put together title teams from elements as diverse as a Democratic ticket."

That was John Wooden.

And that might be one of the best, most complete descriptions of Wooden. To do so in fewer words is nearly impossible. The world's best writers would have difficulty.

Coach. Teacher. Friend. Father. Mentor. Husband. Icon. Winner. Champion. Legend. Wizard. Player. Greatest. Christian. Guru. Counselor. All of those work, but none is complete. Wooden himself always went back to "teacher" more than any other.

The former UCLA coach from Indiana who shaped the game of basketball as much as anyone since Dr. James Naismith, the game's inventor, passed away on the evening of June 4, 2010. Wooden died of natural causes at the Ronald Reagan UCLA Medical Center, where he'd been hospitalized a week earlier because of dehydration. He was less than five months shy of turning 100.

He left behind a legacy that will never be matched.

John Wooden is arguably the greatest coach in the history of sports. Oh, there have been remarkable coaches and managers throughout history such as Vince Lombardi, Casey Stengel, "Bear" Bryant, Adolph Rupp and Dean Smith. You could even throw former Tennessee State University track coach Ed Temple in there. Or, if you're more modern-day, sure Pat Summit, Mike Krzyzewski, Joe Torre and Phil Jackson would make some top-10 lists. But here's the thing. The "modern-day" coaches will tell you how much they've learned, how much they've benefited

Wooden talks with reporters in his office in Los Angeles in March 1972 after he learned he was named The Associated Press' college basketball Coach of the Year for 1972-73—the fifth time he won the award.

from John Wooden, regardless of the sport.

"The way he took great players and molded them into national champions with a sprinkling of overachievers is spectacular," Hall of Fame college football coach Bobby Bowden has said of Wooden.

Although Wooden won't be remembered as basketball's winningest coach, he certainly is the most celebrated and decorated. During a 40-year coaching career at the high school and college ranks, Wooden's teams won 885 games and lost 203.

He won at every level. His Martinsville (Indiana) High School team won the Indiana State championship in 1927. He was the best player on Purdue's national championship squad in 1932. Early in his coaching career, he guided Indiana Teachers College (now Indiana State) to the NAIA national championship game. Then, his practically unbreakable streaks at UCLA: 10 national championships in 12 seasons

(above) Wooden reacts after a technical foul was called during the championship game against Kentucky in San Diego, California on March 31, 1975. (opposite) Wooden wears the basketball net around his neck in celebration after the Bruins won the NCAA basketball championship with a 92-85 victory over Kentucky in San Diego, California on March 31, 1975.

(including seven straight), 38 consecutive NCAA tournament victories, four undefeated seasons (including back-to-back in 1971-72 and 1972-73), and an 88-game winning streak.

Understandably, he was the first person inducted into the Naismith Memorial Basketball Hall of Fame as both a player (1960) and a coach (1973).

But throughout such a remarkable career of winning, success to John Wooden wasn't predicated on whether his team had the higher score at the end of a contest. It was about char-

acter and reputation, and having a life that made a difference.

"Coach Wooden never talked about winning and losing, but rather about the effort to win. He rarely talked about basketball, but generally about life," Hall of Fame player Bill Walton said through a released statement after Wooden's death. "He never talked about strategy, statistics or plays, but rather about people and character. Coach Wooden never tired of telling us that once you become a good person, then you have a chance of becoming a good basketball player."

Walton added: "John Wooden represents the conquest of substance over hype, the triumph of achievement over erratic flailing, the conquest of discipline over gambling, and the triumph of executing an organized plan over hoping that you'll be lucky, hot or in the zone.

"John Wooden also represents the conquest of sacrifice, hard work and commitment to achievement over the pipe dream that someone will just give you something, or that you can take a pill or turn a key to get what you want.

"The joy and happiness in Coach Wooden's life came from the success and accomplishments of others. He never let us forget what he learned from his two favorite teachers, Abraham Lincoln and Mother Theresa, that 'a life not lived for others is not a life.'

"I thank John Wooden every day for all his selfless gifts, his lessons, his time, his vision and especially his faith and patience. This is why our eternal love for him will never fade away. This is why we call him 'Coach.'"

Another former player, Gail Goodrich, echoed Walton's sentiments through his own prepared statement: "Nobody was more beloved than Coach. He loved people, and had this tremendous gift to communicate with everyone, regardless of age or background. He always considered himself a teacher, and a teacher he was. When I played for him, he taught me the game of basketball. Later I came to realize, he really taught me the valuable aspects of life. As competitive as he was both as a player and a coach, he was incorruptible. He lived and taught with a simple philosophy that building a winning team or a successful life can be accomplished without breaking the rules or sacrificing personal values."

Later in his life, a life that didn't slow down much when he retired from coaching in 1975, John Wooden lived every day to its fullest. His beliefs, however, gave him a certain peace about his future. He had a deep Christian faith that he shared, sparingly, with those around him. He didn't push it on others; he always felt religious beliefs were a personal choice. At the same time, though, he quoted verses from the Bible and read from it daily.

That, along with his deep love for his wife Nell, who passed away in 1985, might explain his thoughts on dying. In "Coach Wooden: One-on-One," a 60-day devotional book that Wooden co-authored with former assistant coach Jay Carty, Wooden told the story of the time he was asked, after delivering a speech, if he was afraid to die:

"No, I don't think I am. I'm not going to intentionally hurry it up, but you know, I'm over 90 years of age. I've had a long life. I have a wonderful family and the Lord has let them all be near me. They're never far away. I had 53 wonderful years with Nellie. I've been blessed in so many ways with so many friends. No, I'm not afraid to die. Out yonder somewhere, I'll be with Nellie again, but when?

Wooden stands with two of his former players, Kareem Abdul-Jabbar, left, and Bill Walton during a news conference at the Anaheim Hilton Hotel in Anaheim, California on March 22, 1994. They announced the inaugural NCAA John R. Wooden Classic men's basketball doubleheader, which debuted in December of that year.

Coach John Wooden

Not until after death. But I'm ready."

Wooden's love for Nell, the rest of his family, and God was seen most of all by his players. Hall of Fame player Kareem Abdul-Jabbar (whom Wooden insisted on calling by his birth name, Lewis Alcindor), said in 1999 that Wooden's influence on his personal life "has been most greatly felt in my attempts as a parent."

"Coach Wooden is a pretty clever man," Abdul-Jabbar added. "He figured out how to take the two things that he valued most—family and basketball—to do his life's work and the Lord's work. That's not always easy but he pulled it off.

"There aren't a whole lot of people who can say that."

Then again, there haven't been many people out there like John Wooden.

Each person who has revolutionized his or her craft is recognized by a single name: Shakespeare, Picasso, Hemingway, Elvis. Wooden is on that list.

(above) Legend John Wooden gets a pat on the back from the UCLA mascot as he and head coach Jim Harrick are introduced during halftime of the Purdue-Villanova game in the John Wooden Classic on December 9, 1995. (opposite) UCLA coach John Wooden is shown on the UCLA bench as his team plays.

"He is the greatest coach in the history of basketball," Ben Howland, the first UCLA coach since Wooden to lead the Bruins to back-to-back Final Four appearances in 2006 and 2007, said of Wooden during the weekend of the 2006 Final Four in Indianapolis. "What he accomplished at UCLA in terms of wins and losses will never be equaled again."

To put it simply, there never will be another coach who touches the game of college basketball on and off the court quite like John Wooden. ●

Wooden watches his players during a workout in the Astrodome in Houston, Texas in January 1968. Bruin player Lew Alcindor has the ball.

Basketball Royalty

People couldn't help but stare as the older gentleman was helped to the table in the dark and previously loud ballroom. People stopped what they were doing and stared. The loud rumble turned into a hush. People just wanted to watch him. They didn't want to talk. They didn't want to try to stab more cubed cheese with toothpicks. They didn't want to make any type of commotion. They couldn't, really. They were mesmerized. They just wanted to watch. In many ways, most of the people in the room hadn't seen someone of this magnitude. Frankly, in recent years, if not decades, there haven't been many people in the sports world of John Wooden's magnitude and magnetism.

In sports circles, he was royalty. After all, his UCLA teams won more national championships in a short span (10 in 12 years) than any other basketball team ever had or ever will, especially under one coach.

The stillness at this reception in Indianapolis before the start of the 2000 Final Four didn't last long. Once Wooden reached his table and sat down, hordes of people immediately started lining up next to Wooden, who had his daughter, Nan Muehlhausen, at his side. Folks wanted to meet him, to shake his hand, to have a photo taken with him or to get him to sign anything from a sheet of paper to the back of a dry cleaning ticket.

For many of these people, it was almost as if there was something magical or healing just being in the presence of the "Wizard of Westwood." Incredibly approachable, even in his early 90s at the time, Wooden never batted an eye. As he was known to do, he simply smiled and talked with people, or acquiesced to their requests, as if they were old friends.

To some, when the time seemed right, Wooden would quote poetry. For instance, when one gentleman mentioned that he was a former school teacher, Wooden, a former teacher himself, commended the man and then recited one of his favorite verses:

No written word nor spoken plea
Can teach our youth what they should be.
Nor all the books on all the shelves
It's what the teachers are themselves.

But that was John Wooden. Whether because of his God-fearing nature or his Midwestern roots, John Wooden treated everyone the same. He wasn't a perfect person or even a perfect coach, but he was a far cry from the egotistical, win-at-all-cost attitudes often found in sports today at all levels. His attitude partially came from lessons he received from his father while growing up in Indiana in a setting that wasn't what you'd consider "royal."

Born to Work

Farming never has been an easy occupation. That especially held true in the early 20th century when the work was especially arduous. It also happened to be one of the main jobs for Americans. In fact, according to the United States Department of Agriculture, early in the 20th century,

Wooden was an All-American basketball player for three years, 1930-1932, and Player of the Year in 1932.

41 percent of the nation's workforce worked in agriculture. Joshua Hugh Wooden and his wife Roxie Anna Wooden were two such people.

The couple lived in Hall, Indiana, where Joshua was a tenant farmer – one who works on land owned by someone else – for a landlord named Cash Ludlow. Joshua Wooden wasn't very big in stature, but he was a hard worker, and a strong but gentle man.

Roxie Anna was what many might consider a stereotypical wife of a farmer in the 1920s and '30s. She worked as hard as her husband. And, like Joshua, she did so without complaining. Besides cooking and taking care of the house, she also did all of the washing, ironing, cooking and canning *without* electricity or inside plumbing.

She also gave birth to four boys. The second, born on Friday, October 14, 1910, was John Robert Wooden. (The others were Maurice, who was known as "Cat," Daniel and William.)

Although she loved her boys dearly, Roxie Anna suffered a terrible loss with the death of two daughters, Cordelia, who died of diphtheria at the age of 3; and another who died at birth.

"Mom wanted a daughter desperately, and those two events hurt her more than anything else life threw at her," Wooden wrote in "Coach Wooden: One-on-One." "She carried a sense of loss on her shoulders forever."

In 1918, when John Wooden was about 7, the family moved from Hall to a small white house on a 60-acre farm in the tiny town of Centerton, Indiana, that Roxie Anna inherited from her father. How tiny? At the time, the population of Centerton – located about 12 miles from Hall – was 86.

It was on that farm Wooden learned many of the lessons – mostly from his parents' example – that he carried with him for the rest of his life.

He saw hard work, the majority of which was done without the use of equipment and machines. The Wooden boys also experienced hard work, whether it was milking the cows, picking tomatoes, or weeding and bugging potatoes.

Wooden also learned that one didn't need a lot of material possessions to be happy in this world. That was a common theme for most Depression-era Americans. For Wooden, though, it never left him. That might help explain why he never fought the UCLA administration over his embarrassingly low salary – at least it should be embarrassing for the UCLA administration.

Wooden, who made $6,000 a year when he started at UCLA, was still just making $32,500 when he retired in 1975. To make matters worse, during the first 12 years of his career, his salary was coming from UCLA's student association, which wasn't putting money into a retirement fund for Wooden.

"If I had known that, I never would have come to UCLA," Wooden said. "But I took the job, so I wanted to honor my contract."

Life on the farm in Centerton wasn't all work for the Wooden boys, though. Joshua made sure that his boys had some time to be boys. John Wooden quickly realized, at least as much as an 8-year-old boy can realize, that he had a talent and a love for both baseball and basketball.

For basketball, which was still a relatively young sport at the time, Roxie Anna took one of her black cotton hose, formed it into a ball as best she could, and sewed it up. Meanwhile, Joshua took an old tomato basket, cut out the bottom and nailed it up inside the barn.

The same care went into allowing the boys to play baseball, which emerged as John Wooden's favorite sport. Joshua plowed a baseball diamond for his sons, who whittled their own bats from tree limbs using a knife, file and plane.

"Even in those early years my dreams were entwined with school, basketball, baseball, and college," said Wooden.

But one of the most lasting impressions from those years on the farm in Centerton came when Wooden graduated from Centerton Grade School. That day, Joshua gave

No written word nor spoken plea

Can teach our youth what they should be.

Nor all the books on all the shelves

It's what the teachers are themselves.

–John Wooden

"Johnny," who was decked out in his finest overalls, a two-dollar bill, telling him, "As you long as you keep this you'll never be broke."

He also gave him a small card with something written on both sides. As John Wooden looked at the card, his dad told him, "Son, try and live up to these things."

What things? On one side was a verse by American writer and professor Henry Van Dyke which read:

Four things a man must learn to do
If he would make his life more true:
To think without confusion clearly,
To love his fellow-man sincerely,
To act from honest motives purely,
To trust in God and Heaven securely.

The other side of the card was Joshua Wooden's "seven-point creed."

1. **Be true to yourself.**
2. **Help others.**
3. **Make each day your masterpiece.**
4. **Drink deeply from good books, especially the Bible.**
5. **Make friendship a fine art.**
6. **Build a shelter against a rainy day.**
7. **Pray for guidance and count and give thanks for your blessings every day.**

John Wooden carried that card with him until it wore out. And then he wrote it out again and carried it until that one wore out. And he repeated that process several times throughout the rest of his life. The two-dollar bill he eventually gave to his son Jim.

Although that story and the contents of the card have been written in nearly every book by or about John Wooden, they bear repeating. As he promised his dad, Wooden tried his best to live by those thoughts. He wasn't always successful, but there's a wonderful story that might best display Wooden taking his dad's lessons to heart.

A few days after the 1947-48 season, Wooden's second year of coaching at Indiana State – which was then an NAIA school and had finished as the national tournament's runners-up – two NCAA Division-I programs contacted him about becoming their coach: the University of Minnesota and the University of California-Los Angeles.

After talking with Frank McCormick, the athletics director at Minnesota, and Wilbur Johns, UCLA's athletics director who had also been coaching the basketball team for nine seasons, Wooden was all but set on the Minnesota job. The only hang-up was whether he'd be able to bring his own assistant coach, Ed Powell. Otherwise, he was a Big Ten guy – he was familiar with the schools, he loved the Midwest, all of it meant home for him. Certainly more so than Southern California.

Still, he wanted to think about it. So, Wooden set up phone conversations with each man, within an hour of each other, on the same evening a few days later. He told each that he would give them his answer then.

In an odd twist of fate, a snowstorm struck the Minneapolis area that day. McCormick, who was supposed to call Wooden first, couldn't reach a phone at his specified time. Not knowing about McCormick's predicament, when Johns called Wooden at the designated time, an hour after McCormick, Wooden agreed to become the next coach at UCLA.

About an hour later, McCormick got a hold of Wooden saying that everything was ready for him to take over the Gopher program. Wooden told him that he'd already given Johns and UCLA his word. No amount of persuasion – or the story of the snowstorm – from McCormick could change Wooden's mind. His word was his word. A lesson he learned from his father.

Wooden stands with Kareem Abdul-Jabbar and Bill Walton during a jersey-retiring ceremony at Pauley Pavilion in Los Angeles, California in February 1990.

A Father's Influence

Because an athlete spends so much time with his teammates and coaches, they become an extended family. A true coach, a coach who cares about his athletes at whatever level, is more than someone who gives instruction or sets up plays. A true coach will tell you that his role is to be everything from a mentor, counselor, friend, father and mother to his athletes. That's the way it was for John Wooden, who often said that he realized that lesson more and more each year.

"A coach is a teacher first of all," he said. "He must be a teacher and the teacher must be interested in not just the present but also the future of the youngsters who are under their supervision.

"One of the things I'm most proud of my 27 years at UCLA is the fact that all of my players graduated and practically all have done well in any variety of professions."

(above) Wooden talks with Ed Powell, his assistant at Indiana State, at Wooden's home in Terre Haute, Indiana. (opposite) The tournament namesake sits contentedly in the stands as fans cheer in the closing minutes of UCLA's 69-58 victory over New Mexico in the John Wooden Classic in December 1997.

So much of who John Wooden was came from his parents, in particular, though, his father. Joshua, who was a deeply religious man, read poetry and the Bible every night. Oftentimes he'd read aloud to his family. That influence led to all four of his boys to either major or minor in English during their college careers.

Throughout the rest of his life, John Wooden shared that same love and appreciation of poetry and the Bible, and tried his best to apply lessons from each to his entire life, not just in basketball.

Joshua Wooden would preach to his boys: "Always try to learn from others, because you'll never know a thing that you didn't learn from somebody else — even if it's what not to do."

In 1924, five years before the start of the Great Depression and a year after John Wooden started attending Martinsville High School, the Wooden family lost the 60-acre farm in Centerton. Trying to get through the tough times, Joshua had decided to raise hogs. He borrowed money for everything he'd need for the hogs. Unfortunately, when he vaccinated them for cholera, an intestinal infection common in the early part of the 20th century, the shots ended up giving the hogs the disease and they all died.

Broke, the family moved to nearby Martinsville. Joshua found work at the Homelawn Sanitarium, a health spa, giving massages in the bath house. He worked there for 26 years, until he died in 1950.

(above) Wooden accepts the game ball from Notre Dame coach Digger Phelps after UCLA had set a new consecutive winning streak of 61 games. (opposite) Wooden pauses contemplatively as he takes questions from the media in 2003.

Love at First Sight

No story about John Wooden in the 1920s would be complete without mentioning a chance meeting he had at the school carnival in July 1926. It was there that Johnny Wooden saw Nellie Riley, one of his schoolmates. Wooden, who was shy and awkward around girls, found Riley to be "a pert, vivacious, captivating girl with a very vibrant personality." But, of course, he didn't do anything about it.

Luckily Nellie Riley wasn't as reserved. A few weeks after they spotted each other at the carnival, Nellie talked one of her friends, Mary Schnaiter, and Mary's brother Jack into driving out to the Wooden farm.

When they drove up, Wooden was plowing a field not far from the road. They tried to get his attention. He saw them but acted as if he didn't. He desperately wanted to go over and talk to them, but he just couldn't gather the courage. After a few minutes, Nellie and her friends left. Without Wooden.

Early during the school year a couple months later, Nellie cornered Wooden in the hallway and asked why he didn't walk over to the car that day in July.

"I was all dirty and sweaty," he said. "I thought you'd probably make fun of me."

"Johnny, I would never make fun of you. Never."

John Wooden was in love. So was Nellie Riley. ●

Wooden, newly announced head basketball coach at UCLA, celebrates with his wife, Nell, left, and their children, Nancy, 14, and James, 11, at their home in Terre Haute, Indiana on April 20, 1948.

The "India Rubber Man"

Martinsville High School was like most of the schools in Indiana – in the 1920s as well as today – where basketball was king. The school didn't have a baseball team. At the time, because of a player's death a few years earlier, the school didn't have a football team. So, basically, basketball was it.

Basketball's popularity at Martinsville certainly wasn't hurt by the fact that the school's coach, Glenn Curtis, had won two state championships before Wooden's first year. (Keep in mind that basketball had been born barely 30 years before then, in January 1892.)

Curtis was a coach who cared about his players. He often quoted poetry. And he stressed to his players the importance of practice and getting the details right. Sound familiar?

Wooden made the Martinsville High team as a sophomore in the 1925-26 school year. As he began to excel almost immediately as a basketball player at Martinsville, his dad Joshua would remind him, "Johnny, don't try to be better than somebody else, but never cease trying to be the best you can be. You have control over that. The other you don't."

Wooden did just that. Throughout his playing and coaching careers, as well as throughout his life in general, Wooden always tried to do his best.

During Wooden's time at Martinsville High School, the Artesians reached the championship game of the state tournament all three years. That was no small feat.

At the time, the high school tournament in Indiana was open to 777 schools. There weren't districts or classifications. It was literally a winner-take-all, best-team-in-the-state tournament, whether that meant the biggest school in the state or the smallest. By the time they reached the end, a two-day affair, it definitely became a battle of attrition. The final 16 teams played on Friday night in Indianapolis, with eight advancing to Saturday. In order to be one of the last two teams standing, teams would have to play three games on Saturday – one in the morning, one in the afternoon, and then the championship that night. (Yes, four games in 24 hours.)

In 1926, Wooden's sophomore season, 719 schools signed up to play. In the championship, Martinsville lost to Marion, 30-23. The following season, Martinsville beat Muncie Central, 26-23, for the Indiana state title at the Butler University Field House. The people of Martinsville were so proud of their boys that they gave each player a silver Hamilton pocket watch, which Wooden kept late into his life.

Oddly, if not true to Wooden's personality, winning the championship didn't rank as the most memorable game for Wooden. Instead, the next season's championship contest, once again against Muncie Central, outweighed the 1927 game.

See, on March 17, 1928, Martinsville led the season

John Wooden, who had just accepted a three-year contract to coach at the University of California at Los Angeles, poses at his home in Terre Haute, Indiana on April 20, 1948.

The "India Rubber Man"

finale by one point, 12-11, in the closing minutes. The rules of the game were slightly different then. Instead of taking the ball out of bounds after a basket or a possession change other than a rebound or turnover, the teams would line up for a center jump. And the player jumping was allowed to get his own tip.

After Wooden, who was a guard and the Artesians' best shooter, missed a technical foul shot, the ball went back to midcourt for a center jump.

As Wooden described it in "They Call Me Coach": "Charlie Secrist, the Muncie center, tipped the ball behind him, grabbed it and in a wild, sweeping underhand motion arched the ball toward the basket. ... It seemed to go into the rafters and came straight down the middle of the basket, hardly fluttering the net."

Immediately, Wooden called a timeout. Coach Glenn Curtis set up a play that seemed to work. An Artesian player got off a good shot, but it rolled around the rim and back out.

Muncie Central won, 13-12.

"Losing that game was the most disappointing thing that ever happened to me as a player," Wooden said years later.

Wooden's career was far from over, however.

Being one of the best players in the state of Indiana on one of the best teams in the state, several universities wanted Wooden's services. With any type of national media basically being nonexistent, Wooden was focusing on the in-state schools. Butler, Indiana, Notre Dame and Purdue were the main possibilities.

One school Wooden might have considered briefly — if even that long — was the University of Kansas. To make some money during the summer before his senior year, Wooden and a friend, Carl Holler, hitchhiked throughout the Midwest to harvest wheat. A Kansas alum suggested that Wooden stop by Lawrence and meet with KU coach "Phog" Allen — known today as the "Father of Basketball Coaching" and a man who learned

the game from its inventor, Dr. James Naismith — about possibly playing for the Jayhawks.

Kansas was one of the top college programs in the country even at that time, but it wasn't widely known, not only because of the lack of media coverage but also because there wasn't an NCAA to crown national champions. In 1936 the Helms Athletic Foundation National Championships were awarded to teams retroactively. The Helms Foundation gave the 1922 and '23 championships to the University of Kansas.

Before harvesting wheat throughout Kansas, Nebraska, South Dakota and North Dakota, Wooden and Holler did spend two days working on the crew that was building KU's Memorial Stadium, in which the Jayhawk football team still plays today.

Since Wooden knew he wanted to attend college relatively close to Martinsville, Kansas wasn't really in the mix. That left the local schools. Indiana was the closest to Martinsville, less than 20 miles away, but Purdue had a great engineering program, which is what Wooden wanted to pursue.

So, even though he'd never stepped foot on its campus, Wooden chose to attend Purdue. That also meant the three-time All-State basketball performer would be playing for Ward "Piggy" Lambert, a coach who liked his teams to play an up-tempo style.

Lambert wasn't an intimidating figure, standing just 5-feet-6. Possibly because of his size, most of Lambert's Purdue teams before Wooden were smaller and quicker than their competition. And it worked. During his first five years as Purdue's coach, the Boilermakers won two Big Ten titles. Lambert tweaked his philosophy of smaller players two years before the arrival of Wooden, though, when he got 6-6 center Charles "Stretch" Murphy.

Thanks to Lambert and his style of play — along with Wooden's own God-given ability — Wooden became one of the top players in the country during

Four things a man must learn to do If he would make his life more true:

To think without confusion clearly,
To love his fellow-man sincerely,
To act from honest motives purely,
To trust in God and Heaven securely.

–American writer and
professor Henry Van Dyke

his three varsity seasons at Purdue.

Writer Steve Bisheff worded Wooden's ability perfectly in his book, "John Wooden: An American Treasure": "Wooden was as popular in his time as a Wilt Chamberlain or Michael Jordan would come to be generations later. He was the player everybody talked about, the one all the Indiana kids growing up with hoops in their driveway tried to emulate."

As a player, Wooden was what you would call a "playmaker," before the term meant anything. He was a perfect player for Lambert's system because he was a wonderful ball-handler and an even better hustler. He constantly went after loose balls, diving on the floor or into the seats or into a wall, and drove hard to the basket even if it meant getting hammered by an opponent, only to get right back up as quickly as possible, ready to make something happen. Because of his tenacity and ability to bounce back, he earned the nickname the "India Rubber Man."

"He was one of the best dribblers ever," said Eddie Powell, who remembered Wooden as a player at Purdue before playing for him at South Bend Central a few years later. "He could control the dribble or give you the speed dribble. He could dribble the ball down the floor faster than the rest of us could run without the ball.

"He wasn't fancy, but he was fundamentally sound."

Wooden worked great with Murphy as the two formed one of college basketball's best outside-inside combos during the first half of the century.

By the time his collegiate career was over, Wooden scored 475 points in 48 games. He averaged 12.2 points per game in his senior year. (Remember, this was at a time when teams commonly scored in the 30s.)

In his first year, 1929-30, Wooden helped lead the Boilermakers to one of their best seasons as they went undefeated in Big Ten play en route to the conference championship. They finished the season with an overall mark of 13-2. Incidentally, Wooden missed the two games that Purdue lost that year because of a leg injury he suffered in a car accident in December. Wooden took the coincidence in stride.

"I certainly don't want people to misinterpret this," Wooden said, "but I've been told that our 1929-30 team would have gone undefeated had I not injured my leg."

Wooden, as he would end up doing all three seasons at Purdue, was a first-team All-American selection in 1930.

His best season, however, as a player – as well as Purdue's best season – came two years later, when Wooden was a senior.

Still seven years from a national tournament to determine the NCAA's champion, the Boilermakers went 17-1 in 1932 and were selected by the Helms Foundation as the national champs.

Oddly, much like the 1930 season when the two losses came after Wooden missed games because of injuries from a car accident, the only loss Purdue suffered in '32 was after Wooden was in a car accident.

Riding with Piggy Lambert on the way to playing Illinois in January, Wooden cut his hand on broken glass after Lambert skidded on a patch of ice and the car overturned. Wooden played against the Illini in the 28-21 loss, but he was certainly at less than 100 percent.

After the season, in addition to the Boilermakers being selected as the national champions and Wooden being picked as an All-American again, Wooden won the player of the year award from the All-America Board of Basketball.

Although Martinsville coach Glenn Curtis had a tremendous impact on Wooden, and much of Wooden's coaching characteristics came from Curtis, Lambert is the one who can be credited for helping mold Wooden into a legendary coach.

Lew Alcindor towers over his coach, who has some words of advice for the UCLA star during a workout in March 1969 in Louisville, Kentucky.

The "India Rubber Man"

Lambert's use of quickness throughout his coaching career, even with taller players such as "Stretch" Murphy, stuck with Wooden as did his approach to the fast-break offense. Of course, in order to maximize quickness and the fast break, teams have to be well-conditioned. Another lesson learned from Lambert.

"The greatest influence on me both from the standpoint of playing and coaching," Wooden said of Lambert. "Coach Lambert had a fetish for details."

Fittingly, John Wooden, Ward "Piggy" Lambert and Charles "Stretch" Murphy all were inducted into the Naismith Memorial Basketball Hall of Fame in 1960, in its second class.

John Wooden, The Student

Basketball wasn't Wooden's only strength in college. He was an exceptional student, originally wanting to pursue a career in engineering. And, he had an uncanny ability of finding ways to make money.

At that time, schools did not offer athletic scholarships, although coaches usually helped their athletes find jobs to help pay their tuition. Plus, with Joshua Wooden's meager income from the Homelawn Sanitarium, John needed to help support his family during the Depression Era.

"Piggy" Lambert helped Wooden on the tuition front. He helped Wooden get a job waiting tables and washing dishes at the Beta fraternity house. Wooden also worked in the Purdue athletic department, mainly taping athletes in the training room.

Wooden, however, did have an intriguing offer that would have made his college life a little easier. Shortly before Wooden's sophomore season, Lambert told him that a Lafayette doctor offered to pay for the last three years of his college education. Such an arrangement wasn't against the rules at that time, but through Lambert's counseling – which included implying that it

was better for Wooden to work through college – Wooden declined the offer.

A few years later, Lambert's counseling would force Wooden to follow his conscience once again. When Wooden graduated from Purdue, he had a chance to barnstorm with the New York Celtics for $5,000, which is more than three times the $1,500 he would have gotten for teaching English, coaching four sports and serving as the athletic director at a high school. After talking with Lambert, though, and being reminded that he attended Purdue to receive an education, Wooden knew that deep down he wanted to teach and coach, even if it meant taking that $1,500 a year.

Declining the doctor's offer for a "free ride" to Purdue meant that Wooden would have to come up with other ways to earn the desperately needed money. For Wooden that wasn't a problem.

For instance, he came up with a clever idea of getting stores to donate black and gold ribbons (Purdue's colors) and some safety pins. Then he'd make and sell lapel pins.

"Stretch" Murphy was a profitable help to Wooden, as well. "Stretch" had a gig where he copied the rosters and stats for both teams and had high school students sell them to fans at Boilermaker basketball games. He eventually turned the business of selling this early version of game programs over to Wooden, who made a nickel for every dime program that was sold. During the football season, Wooden sold football programs.

The Boilermakers had a huge football rivalry at the time with the University of Chicago. Each year the teams played at Soldier Field in Chicago, and there was such a huge Purdue fan base that traveled to the game that the Monon Railroad had the "Monon Hoosier Express" that

Wooden poses with players Swen Nater and Bill Walton in 1972.

ran from Lafayette to Chicago. Murphy sold concessions aboard the train. It was another business that he turned over to his best friend Wooden, who'd tell people that he was going to "walk to Chicago." (He was walking up and down the aisles of the train, selling everything from food, to soft drinks, to cigarettes.)

Between basketball and working, Wooden still found plenty of time to work hard at getting a good education. Of course, although his father taught him the importance of education, Wooden found some extra motivation early during his time at Purdue.

He learned during his freshman year that students who made the Dean's honor roll list received free tuition during the spring semester. Since scholarships weren't given in those days to athletes of any caliber, to save the spring semester's 75-dollar fee, Wooden studied harder to make sure he made the Dean's list.

It paid off, literally and figuratively. He was 19th out of 4,675 in his graduating class of 1932. He also received the Big Ten Conference medal for being the league's top scholar and athlete. That award meant as much to Wooden as anything else he accomplished during his four years at Purdue.

There is one interesting side note to Wooden's time at Purdue. Years later, he told writer Steve Bisheff that if he had to do it over again, he might not have selected Purdue.

"If I had been given better high school counseling, I would have gone to Indiana University," Wooden said in Bisheff's book, "John Wooden: An American Treasure".

The main reason for the change of heart?

To receive the engineering degree at Purdue, Wooden

Wooden sits behind the NCAA's Theodore Roosevelt Award at the conclusion of the NCAA's Honors Dinner in Dallas, Texas in January 1996. The NCAA's highest award is presented annually to a distinguished citizen.

would have needed to attend an unpaid "civil engineering camp" every summer, which would have eliminated his ability to work and earn money to help support his family. So, he became a Liberal Arts major with an emphasis in English.

"From that point on, I knew I would probably be a teacher," Wooden added in Bisheff's book. "As Lincoln said: 'Things work out best for those who make the best of the way things work out.'" ●

Wonders & Wonders

1. Be true to yourself.

2. Help others.

3. Make each day your masterpiece.

4. Drink deeply from good books, especially the Bible.

5. Make friendship a fine art.

6. Build a shelter against a rainy day.

7. Pray for guidance and count and give thanks for your blessings every day.

—Joshua Wooden's
"Seven-Point Creed"

John Wooden holds the Major College Coach of the Year Award and Lucias Mitchell of Kentucky State holds the Small College coaching award during the National Association of Basketball Coaches Awards Dinner in Washington, D.C. on March 20, 1970.

Nell, A Ruptured Appendix & Freddie Stalcup

Between his junior and senior years at Purdue, in 1931, John Wooden had a chance to go to the United States Military Academy at West Point, which, back then, included four more years of eligibility. Oh, the offer was tempting for Wooden, who had served in the National Guard in high school.

There was just one minor problem: Nell Riley. Although there had not been an official proposal of marriage, they had long known that they would be married when John finished college. So, as tempting as four years at West Point was to Wooden, it was equally appalling to Nell.

"I agreed to wait these four years," she said. "You go, but I'll wait no longer."

That's all Wooden needed to hear. No West Point for him. But it meant that he and Nell could begin planning for the rest of their lives.

Since money was tight for the Wooden family, John and Nell knew that they would have to pay for their wedding and beyond. There wouldn't be any type of nest egg waiting for them when he graduated the next year from Purdue.

One way Wooden knew he could make money relatively fast was playing some type of professional basketball, even though he declined the New York Celtics' $5,000 offer to barnstorm.

Gaining wild popularity in the upper Midwest as a basketball star, Wooden caught the eye of George Halas, the founder of the Chicago Bears, who owned a professional basketball team, the Chicago Bruins. Wooden accepted an offer from Halas to play in three playoff games at $100 each.

Wooden saved that $300 as well as some more throughout that summer from barnstorming in preparation for his August 8 wedding day. By that time, Wooden had also accepted a job for the fall at Dayton High School in Kentucky to teach English, serve as the athletic director, and coach basketball, baseball, football and track.

Two days beforehand, on August 6, 1932, he went to the Martinsville Trust Company to withdraw his life savings of $909.05. The bank was closed. Permanently. Nearly a month earlier, on July 8, the Dow Jones reached its lowest point of the Great Depression (and its lowest average since 1897).

Wooden was understandably devastated.

The next day, Cliff Schnaiter, the father of Mary Schnaiter, the girl whom Nell talked into driving out to the Wooden farm that hot summer day during high school, gave Wooden an envelope containing $200 to help John and Nell. It worked.

On August 8, 1932, John and Nell Wooden were married.

Dayton High School

There's an idea that great athletes make lousy coaches. Eventually in his career, John Wooden would be the exception to that belief. But not at Dayton High School. Really, it's a wonder that Wooden stayed in coaching after that first season.

John Wooden and his wife, Nell, had a special bond long before they were able to get married.

Actually, in football he didn't make it through half of a season.

Wooden knew he was in over his head in football. He never played the sport growing up, so before school started he tried to get a crash course in Football 101 from Purdue head coach Noble Kizer.

Not only did he lack the football skills and knowledge to coach the Green Devils, but Wooden also lacked the patience necessary to lead the team. During the first week of practice, one of the linemen decided to test Wooden's authority. The two got in each other's face and, instead of calmly diffusing the situation with words as Wooden would later be known to do during confrontations, he resorted to pushing and shoving. The altercation ended quickly and the team went back to practicing.

Before the season really got started, although not because of the rift with the lineman, Wooden asked the school superintendent, O.W. Davis, to find his replacement as head coach.

Wooden's basketball coaching career didn't start much better. During his first season, Wooden led the Green Devils to a 6-11 overall record. It would be the only time during his basketball career as a player or a coach that he would be involved with a team that had a losing record.

During the season, though, he saw why great athletes usually don't make good coaches.

"I not only saw my temper flare up," Wooden said, "but I was too critical, impatient, eager to fill players full of information, and quickly irritated when they couldn't absorb it. Since every had come easily for me as a player, I didn't understand why these young men couldn't do the same.

"I had yet to learn that the greatest motivator is a well-deserved pat on the back from someone you respect. Instead, I was quick to criticize, slow to commend.

"I was just a terrible coach."

The next year went well enough that halfway through the basketball season, Wooden was offered a teaching and coaching job at South Bend Central High School in his home state of Indiana. There he would teach English and coach basketball, baseball and tennis.

It was at South Bend where Wooden really began to come into his own as a head coach. He didn't win state championships but he started to successfully develop his coaching style. He even learned an invaluable lesson that sometimes players can step up and surprise their coach.

Before a big weekend with games on Friday and Saturday against Emerson and Fort Wayne Central, Eddie Pawelski told Wooden that he was thinking about quitting the team because he wasn't getting a chance to play. Wooden didn't want that because, even though Pawelski wasn't even good enough to be a backup guard on the basketball team, he was one of Wooden's star baseball players.

In one of those moments when you say something and immediately wonder if you really just said that, Wooden told Pawelski that he would start him against Fort Wayne Central. Start him? Start him? Wooden didn't even want to start Pawelski during a scrimmage in practice, let alone in such a big game.

Figuring he could set the table for Pawelski to fail by making him guard Bill Armstrong, who would go on to become an All-American at Indiana, Wooden sat back and watched. He was shocked by what he saw.

Pawelski "literally took (Armstrong) apart." Pawelski held Armstrong to 12 points, while scoring 12.

"Eddie never sat on the bench again except to rest," Wooden said. "He started every game and was named the most valuable player that year and again the following year as a senior.

"Why I ever said I would start him is still a mystery to me. I had other kids come to me many times after that and ask the same question, but I never appeased another one — at least in that respect."

"A coach is a teacher first of all," he said. "He must be a teacher and the teacher must be interested in not just the present but also the future of the youngsters who are under their supervision. One of the things I'm most proud of my 27 years at UCLA is the fact that all of my players graduated and practically all have done well in any variety of professions.

—John Wooden

One of those kids was Sidney Wicks, who played for Wooden and the Bruins during 1969-71. Wicks was one of the most athletically gifted players during Wooden's career. He also might take the award for pestering Wooden more than any other player ever did. As a sophomore, Wicks felt he should have been starting ahead of either Curtis Rowe or Lynn Shackelford. At the same time, Wicks was slow to understand Wooden's team concept. This time, Wooden didn't give in, and Wicks spent much of his sophomore season on the bench next to Wooden.

Wicks' badgering of Wooden did pay off for the Bruins during the 1970 championship game against Jacksonville and its dominating big man, 7-foot-2 Artis Gilmore. By this time, his junior year, Wicks was starting. The Bruins quickly found themselves down 14-6 early against Jacksonville. During a timeout, Wicks began his plea.

"Coach, you gotta let me play behind that guy."

"You can't guard him from behind, Sidney," Wooden replied in a "you're crazy" kind of tone.

"Yes I can. I'll show you."

Without an obvious alternative, Wooden acquiesced. In much the same way that Pawelski surprised Wooden, Wicks stunned everyone by shutting down Gilmore for the rest of the game. Gilmore ended with 19 points, while Wicks pitched in 17 for UCLA. The Bruins won 80-69.

Wicks was a first-team All-American during his junior and senior seasons.

"His next two years he was the best college forward in the country," Wooden said on the 2007 HBO documentary, "The UCLA Dynasty". "Of course, he would tell you that he was (the best) that other year, too."

"I don't know what would've happened if I'd gone somewhere other than UCLA," Wicks said. "I probably would've scored a lot of points, but I never would have understood how to win. I realize now he was right about me. The things Coach said about my game when I first got here, he was right. If I'd gone somewhere else, I wouldn't have had everything I had at UCLA.

"Hey, I'm a lucky guy. Playing for UCLA back then, having John Wooden coach you, with those great games at Pauley and all those others on national television…hey, it just doesn't get any better than that."

As for Pawelski, that moment with Wooden may have altered his life. Pawelski, who was headed to Indiana to play, enlisted in World War II, where he was shot down in a B-24 raid. Wounded, he wouldn't play basketball again. However, Eddie Pawelski, who changed his last name to Powell, became Wooden's assistant coach at Indiana State and then at UCLA before becoming the head coach at Loyola.

Coincidentally, remember the story about how Wooden ended up at UCLA instead of the University of Minnesota? That assistant coach whom Wooden insisted on taking to Minnesota was Powell. So, in some ways, you can thank Powell for Wooden ending up in Westwood.

As for John and Nell, who now had two children, Nancy and Jim, their first decade of marriage went pretty smoothly. That is, until 1942. With the United States' entry into World War II after Pearl Harbor, John Wooden felt a patriotic duty to serve the country. He was 31 when he enlisted in the Navy – much to Nellie's chagrin.

See, Wooden didn't tell Nell that he enlisted until after the fact. He later said that it was the only time she was "furious" with him.

Before Wooden entered the Navy, Reverend Frank Davidson, one of Wooden's friends and a man who ran an interfaith men's club, gave Wooden a small cross. It wasn't a good luck piece or anything like that, but it served as a reminder of his faith in Jesus Christ.

Wooden and Gene Bartow of Memphis State University at a press conference on March 26, 1973 in St. Louis, Missouri prior to their NCAA championship game.

Wooden often said the following poem was a great way to describe that cross:

I carry a cross in my pocket,
A simple reminder to me of the fact
That I am a Christian wherever I may be;
This little cross is not magic, nor is it
A good luck charm,
It isn't meant to protect me from every
Physical harm;
It's not for identification for all the
World to see,
It's simply an understanding between
My savior and me;
When I put my hand in my pocket to bring
Out a coin or a key,
The cross is there to remind me of the
Price he paid for me;
It reminds me, too, to be thankful for my
Blessings day by day, and to strive
To serve Him better in all that I do
And say;
It is also a daily reminder of the peace
And comfort I share with all who know
My Master and give themselves to His care;
So I carry a cross in my pocket reminding
Me, no one but me, that Jesus Christ is
The Lord of my life if only I will let
Him be.

When Wooden returned to coaching after the War, he kept the cross in his pocket, clutching it during games. Nell had an identical cross that she would grasp during games and eventually be buried with.

"It probably is a good thing for officials that I had that in my hand when a bad call was made," Wooden quipped.

Wooden temporarily stopped his coaching duties as the family moved around with the Navy to Chapel Hill, North Carolina; Iowa City, Iowa; and St. Simons Island, Georgia.

Freddie Stalcup

The name Freddie Stalcup might not be familiar to most people. He wasn't John Wooden's teammate or one of Coach's players, although he was a friend and fraternity brother at Purdue. (He also played football for the Boilermakers.)

But if it weren't for a bad appendix, the only thing the world might know about John Wooden today is that he was a great basketball player. Instead, we don't know as much about Stalcup.

While stationed in Iowa City, Wooden received orders to report to the U.S.S. *Franklin* in the South Pacific. However, he became incredibly ill, only to find out that his appendix would have to be removed. At the time, Navy regulations refused to allow someone at sea for 30 days after certain medical procedures, such as an appendectomy.

So, Wooden's orders were changed and Stalcup took his place on the *Franklin*. On March 19, 1945, about 50 miles from Japan, the Japanese bombed the Franklin. Stalcup's gun position — which presumably would've been Wooden's — was hit by a kamikaze. Although the *Franklin* didn't sink, 724 men died that day, including Fred Stalcup Jr. ●

Wooden is shown in Los Angeles, California in January 1970.

DePaul coach Ray Meyer and former UCLA coach John Wooden chat warmly during pre-game ceremonies honoring Meyer's 42-year career in Rosemont, Illinois on March 10, 1984.

A Legend Begins His Legacy

Shortly before Christmas in 1945, Wooden returned home from the Navy. When school resumed in January 1946, Wooden was given his job back as basketball coach.

He was one of the lucky ones.

Many of his friends and colleagues weren't as lucky in the post-War South Bend. It made Wooden mad enough that he began to entertain job offers that spring that would take him away from South Bend Central, and even possibly out of coaching.

"Several job offers seemed to come to me all at once," Wooden said. "There were some opportunities in public relations, another with a fine book publishing company, and some college and good high school coaching offers."

(Incidentally, Wooden did work part-time for Harcourt Brace Publishing, but he turned down offers to work for the company full-time.)

After compiling a 218-42 record in 11 years at the high school ranks, Wooden decided to take the job as head basketball and baseball coach and athletic director at Indiana State University, replacing his old coach and mentor, Glenn Curtis, who decided to coach a new professional team.

During his first year, 14 of his 15 players were freshmen.

Breaking Barriers

The National Association of Intercollegiate Athletics (NAIA) has a proud basketball championship history going back to its days as the National Association of Intercollegiate Basketball (NAIB) in 1940 which gave small colleges a chance to compete for a national basketball championship. Eight years later, in 1948, according to the NAIA's website, "the NAIB became the first national organization to offer post-season opportunities to black student-athletes."

Any guesses on the coach who helped that change take place?

Indiana State Teachers College's John Wooden.

Wooden led the Sycamores to a record of 18-7 in his first season as their head coach. That was good enough to receive an invitation to play in the NAIA's national tournament in Kansas City. The NAIA, however, wouldn't allow Wooden to bring reserve player Clarence Walker, who was black. Wooden refused to attend the tournament under those conditions.

By avoiding the tournament, Wooden wasn't necessarily making a stand or forcing the NAIA's hand. To him it was a matter of the team being together, making everyone feel like they were important to the big picture.

In a broad sense, his attitude was similar to the family in the movie "Home Alone," which stressed that same importance.

The Sycamores were scheduled to fly to New York to

After compiling a 218-42 record in 11 years at the high school ranks, Wooden decided to take the job as head basketball coach, head baseball coach, and athletic director at Indiana State University in 1946.

A Legend Begins His Legacy

play at Madison Square Garden. Because of his experience in being shot down in a B-24 during the War, Jim Powers refused to fly.

"There's no way I'm getting on a plane," Powers told Wooden. "You can go without me, but I'm not flying."

"Coach refused to leave me behind – got station wagons and we drove out to New York," Powers said later. "It was family; nobody got left behind. … His concern for us went way beyond basketball. We were part of a family."

His players also learned another valuable lesson on the way to New York: Wooden could be tough. During that drive, the starters were with Wooden in one station wagon and the trainer was with the reserves in the other station wagon. Any time they stopped for food, Wooden ordered for everyone.

"I think it was in Virginia," said Lenny Rzeszewski, a starter, who played for Wooden at South Bend and Indiana State. "We had a meal that didn't satisfy a lot of the individuals, so the other car decided to stop and get some lunch meat and bread. They ate it on the way. That night (Wooden) was so upset with what they did, not following his orders, well, he didn't play anyone else but the five starters."

In 1948, when Indiana State finished the season with a 29-7 mark, the Sycamores received another invitation to play in the NAIA tournament. This time, the NAIA allowed Walker to join the team, thus becoming the first integrated national tournament.

The Sycamores made a good showing at the tournament in Kansas City's Municipal Auditorium, which has hosted more NAIA national tournaments and more NCAA Final Fours than any other venue. Indiana State reached the championship game, only to lose to Louisville.

Still, Wooden was proving to everyone, including the nation's bigger schools, that at the age of 37, he was a viable head coach.

As we know, Minnesota and UCLA both contacted Wooden at the conclusion of the 1948 season, and Wooden chose UCLA in somewhat of a fluke, and signed a three-year contract.

Understandably, the Wooden family was somewhat reluctant about the move, even after going to Southern California. Going from the Midwest to California, for someone entrenched in the Midwest's values complete with his own homespun philosophies, it was like going from Paradise to Sodom and Gomorrah.

It didn't help that UCLA wasn't exactly a basketball school, or even a blip on fans' radar screens. UCLA, which went through a stretch of losing 42 consecutive games to cross-town rival USC, boasted an all-time record of 281-281 before the 1948-49 season.

Not to mention, the conditions of the facilities were less than ideal in the gym that lived up to its nickname of the "B.O. Barn."

"It was hard when I came here," Wooden said. "I had to sweep the floor every day. We had no private dressing rooms. … We had tin lockers. There was wrestling at one end of the gym, gymnastics at another, and at times, a trampoline on the side."

In 1955, the fire marshal wouldn't allow more than 1,300 fans in the old barn, which held nearly twice that. So, the Bruins played their "home" games everywhere but home – the Los Angeles Sports Arena, the Long Beach Arena, and a community college in Santa Monica.

(The popularity of UCLA basketball under Wooden eventually helped the Bruins move into the state-of-the-art Pauley Pavilion, on the UCLA campus, in time for the 1965-66 season.)

In spite of the conditions, Wooden, in somewhat quick fashion, turned things around. During UCLA's first season under Wooden, the Bruins finished with a then-school-record 22 wins against seven losses. They also won the conference.

"This helped me to become more at ease in an area

"Goodness gracious, sakes alive!"

-the closest John Wooden really ever came to cussing as recalled by his 1960s players

where the lifestyle was somewhat foreign to me," said Wooden. "The players accepted me and a new philosophy of fast-break basketball, to which they had never been accustomed, in a fine manner and truly gave their best."

The Bruins continued to improve and play consistent basketball. In Wooden's second year, they won 24 games and reached the NCAA tournament for the first time in school history. They were also the program's first back-to-back winning seasons since 1930 and '31.

In the back of Wooden's mind, as much excitement as he was seeing around the UCLA program, he and Nell weren't at home in California.

At the end of the 1950 season, Piggy Lambert retired from Purdue. The school's administration wanted one of Lambert's own, one of their own, to take over. They offered

(above) John Wooden is congratulated by Jacksonville coach Joe Williams after UCLA beat the Dolphins, 80-69, in the 32nd NCAA Men's Basketball championship at College Park, Maryland on March 21, 1970, giving UCLA their fourth consecutive NCAA championship. (opposite) Bob Myers, Associated Press Sports Editor in Los Angeles, presents the Associated Press trophy to Wooden on behalf of his team at a banquet on the UCLA campus honoring the team in Los Angeles, California.

everything in Lafayette to Wooden in hopes that he'd return.

He would get nearly double the salary he was receiving at UCLA, a new car each year, a five-year contract with raises, a country club membership, a home, and a life insurance policy.

"It was almost unimaginable what Purdue offered," Wooden said.

As fast as he could, he set up a meeting with UCLA athletic director Wilbur Johns and Bill Ackerman, the head of the Associated Students Union, who was, basically, Wooden's boss. He requested that they allow him to leave UCLA. Of course, they didn't let Wooden out of his contract, saying that he needed to honor his third year, the third year that he insisted on in the first place.

"I would never sign another three-year contract again," Wooden said later. "Deeply disappointed, I reported back to Nell and promised we'd simply wait one year until my contract was up, then take the offer from Purdue and move back home where we belonged."

Purdue didn't wait for Wooden. And no other Big Ten schools were calling.

"California was going to be our permanent home," he said.

The first 13 seasons on a national scale, at least, weren't wildly successful. Sure, the Bruins reached the national tournament three times in the 1950s, but they won their opening-round game only once in that stretch.

Wooden was growing frustrated, mainly with himself, but he continued to hone his practices, particularly before the 1960-61 season, which became more important than the games. They became better orchestrated, with a wiser use of the reserve players, a "privilege" for the players to take part in.

"We'd have had a little better chance in earlier years," Wooden conceded in 2007, "if I'd known a little more."

"Coach ran the same drills with the same emphasis every day," said former player Larry Farmer, who played for the Bruins during 1971-73. "The drills that we ran on October the 15th, the first day of practice, we ran on the night before we played for the national championship."

Of course, they worked hard in those practices. Wooden and his assistant coaches would sit down for two hours each morning and map out that afternoon's practice. In essence, they choreographed what former UCLA (and now legendary) announcer Dick Enberg used to call the "Bruin ballet."

And this normally meek, genteel Midwestern man would turn into a tough coach. Not in a yelling, profane-laden way, but as a stern task-master. Really, the closest he really ever came to cussing was when he'd say "Goodness gracious, sakes alive!" But that was enough for the Bruins.

"When you heard those words, you knew all hell was coming next," said Gail Goodrich, who was one of the cogs for the Bruins from 1963-65.

Goodrich was a freshman when the Bruins finally broke through in 1962. That year, for the first time in school history, they reached the Final Four. In the semifinal game in Louisville, Kentucky, UCLA lost to the University of Cincinnati, 72-70, when Tom Thacker hit a last-second shot, his only points of the game. (UCLA lost to Wake Forest, 82-80, in the consolation game.)

But the stage had been set.

There is some debate about why this came to be, whether it was Wooden's decision solely or the suggestion of assistant coach Jerry Norman, but Wooden decided to implement the zone press heading into the 1962-63 season. He had used it sparingly throughout his coaching career, but he never really felt comfortable with the personnel. But this Bruin team featured the likes of Walt Hazzard, Fred Slaughter, Keith Erickson, Jack Hirsch, and Goodrich. ●

Wooden & WORDS

"Coach Wooden didn't talk about winning – ever. His message was to give the game the best you've got. 'That's the goal,' he would tell us. 'Do that and you should be happy. If enough of you do it, our team will be a success.'"

– Dave Meyers, who played on two national championship teams during his time at UCLA, 1973-75

Villanova University basketball coach Jack Kraft congratulates Wooden after the Bruins defeated Villanova 68-62 to win their fifth straight NCAA championship in Houston, Texas on March 27, 1971.

The Pyramid of Success

At first glance it looks like an oversized knock-off food pyramid or a busy set of building blocks. "Building" actually might be the best word to describe John Wooden's famed "Pyramid of Success."

In essence, the Pyramid of Success is the tool Wooden started designing in 1933 to help explain to his students and athletes the characteristics he felt were needed to become successful.

Wooden long felt success was not defined by wins and losses but by the inner knowledge that you gave your best.

"You can fool everyone else," he said, "but in the final analysis only you know whether you goofed off or not."

"Coach Wooden didn't talk about winning – ever," said Dave Meyers, who played on two national championship teams during his time at UCLA, 1973-75. "His message was to give the game the best you've got. 'That's the goal,' he would tell us. 'Do that and you should be happy. If enough of you do it, our team will be a success.'"

Building the Pyramid

As Wooden was thinking about his definition of success in 1933, he wanted more than just to define the word. He wanted to show how, whether in basketball or in life, someone could become successful. A means to the end, so to speak.

Combining a picture of a ladder that his high school coach Glenn Curtis sometimes used before a game to show the steps the Artesians needed to take to win that night, along with knowledge he gained at Purdue of the Great Pyramid of Giza, Wooden set out to build his Pyramid of Success.

"At first, I didn't know how many 'blocks' it would contain, what the blocks would consist of, or in what order they would be positioned," he said. "All I knew was that success would be found at the apex and that each block leading to the top would represent a personal quality necessary for getting there. The Pyramid's blocks and tiers would be my specific directions on how those under my supervision could achieve success by realizing their own potential, both individually and as part of a team.

"Along the way, I came to see that it would also provide the directions for my own coaching – a leadership guidebook – offering a code of conduct for those given the privilege of leading others into the competitive arena."

Over time – almost 15 years – Wooden adjusted the blocks and experimented until he finally came up with 15 fundamental values to use as blocks, while putting them in an order that made the most sense to him. He finally finished the Pyramid of Success toward the end of his tenure at Indiana State and beginning of his time at UCLA.

Without Wooden's guidance, trying to explain the Pyramid of Success is like trying to fathom how the Great Pyramids were built (and still stand today) or the mean-

Wooden holds the NCAA championship trophy, which the Bruins won for the fifth straight year by defeating Villanova University, 68-62, in Houston, Texas on March, 27, 1971. Forward Sidney Wicks (35) wears the basket net around his neck in celebration.

ing of the Bible's book of Revelation. Several writers and speakers have tried over the years, many with some success. So, in 2003, Wooden and one of his co-authors, Steve Jamison, wrote a children's book, "Inch and Miles: The Journey to Success," which helps explain Wooden's theory to kids. Then, in 2005, Wooden and another of his co-authors, former Bruin assistant coach Jay Carty, wrote the book "Coach Wooden's Pyramid of Success."

The following poem, written by Willie Naulls, who played for Wooden at UCLA during 1954-56, appeared in the Wooden-Carty book. It helps explain the principles of the Pyramid from someone who learned them from the designer and has lived them.

"Coach John Wooden of Westwood:
A Messenger on Call"

Coach John Wooden of Westwood has a message for all.

Industriousness and enthusiasm, the cornerstones of his call.

Focused on friendship and loyalty, he stresses cooperation

And mastery of intentness of initiative through self-controlled participation.

Not to forget alertness and condition in developing team spirit's skill

Of maturing competitive greatness, poise and confidence to fulfill.

Inspired by sincerity of ambition and an honest desire to be "as He, men and women can achieve their best through responsible adaptability.

Reliability on the resourcefulness possessed in integrity's might

Is the victory of the good fight of faith, through patience's insight.

So the message of life, of Coach Wooden's call —

SUCCESS is a reward to anyone who gives his all.

For many of the players, the Pyramid of Success didn't mean a lot at the time. After college, it took shape.

"When I sat across the table from David Stern and his five or six attorneys involved in collective-bargaining negotiations for the referees in the NBA, I never felt we were unable to deal with the pressure and animosity … because of John Wooden, because of the Pyramid of Success," said Fred Slaughter, who eventually earned his law degree and became an agent after playing for UCLA, 1962-64.

With the success of Wooden's teams at UCLA, and more of his former players using the Pyramid in their everyday lives, the Pyramid's popularity spread. A window into the soul of the man, they thought.

Eventually, the Pyramid became as well known as Wooden's UCLA teams because it transcended sports. It could be applied to any aspect of a person's life.

People would write letters to Wooden, asking for copies of it. Oftentimes, when someone would send something – a photograph, book, basketball, whatever – to Wooden for his autograph, he would also send back a signed copy of the Pyramid of Success. Copies also were given away through his television show and various magazine articles. Wooden likely gave away at least tens of thousands of copies of the Pyramid over the years.

"I have to admit, I had no idea it would get this much exposure. It's very surprising to me," Wooden said. "It helped me become a better teacher. I think it gave many of my athletes something to aspire to, besides being just a top scorer or respected scholar. I think, overall, the Pyramid epitomizes what I've tried to teach through the years. I'm very proud of it." ●

Wooden & Words

"Coach Wooden came through as a well-read, genuinely caring man. People would always tell me that they cared about me, but I felt Mr. Wooden really meant it. I came out of his office knowing I was going to UCLA."

—Kareem Abdul-Jabbar

The Wizard of Westwood

The moniker seemed appropriate. "The Wizard of Westwood." Funny, albeit not surprisingly so, John Wooden wasn't a fan of the term that many used to describe him. Shoot, he didn't even remotely embrace it.

"Oh, please, don't call me that," he said. "I've never been any type of wizard."

But, John Wooden came pretty close to being a wizard. With a rolled-up program instead of a wand, Wooden went against the norm. He didn't break down every Bruin opponent or focus on winning and losing. In only a few instances did he point out specific opposing players the Bruins would be facing. And he didn't recruit, certainly not actively.

Just look at part of Wooden's 1964 team. Fred Slaughter, an important member of the squad, was recruited to UCLA as a track decathlete, from Topeka, Kansas. With neither coach wanting to waste a full scholarship, Keith Erickson was offered a half scholarship in both basketball and baseball at UCLA. Walt Hazzard, who was from Philadelphia, walked into Wooden's office one day and introduced himself and said he wanted to play basketball. Gail Goodrich's dad, who played at Southern California, became so upset that the Trojans didn't recruit his son because he was small that he encouraged Gail Jr. to attend UCLA. Jack Hirsch played two years of junior-college ball, but wasn't a big-time recruit for any major school. Doug McIntosh was headed to the University of Tennessee until they fired coach John Sines, who told his friend John Wooden about McIntosh, whose parents had moved to

Los Angeles during his senior year of high school.

That team won UCLA's first basketball national championship in 1964.

One of the most famous Bruins – heck, one of the greatest basketball players of all-time – Lew Alcindor (later Kareem Abdul-Jabbar) wrote a letter to Wooden after the Bruins won their first two titles saying he wanted to play for UCLA. His other top schools were the University of Michigan and St. John's, both highly successful programs at the time, and Columbia.

When Alcindor first visited the UCLA campus, however, and met Wooden, his fate was sealed.

"I'd heard a lot about this man and his basketball wisdom," Abdul-Jabbar wrote in his autobiography "Giant Steps," "but he surely did look like he belonged in a one-room schoolhouse.

"He was calm, in no hurry to impress me with his knowledge or his power. He could have made me cool my heels, or jumped up and been my buddy, but he clearly worked on his own terms, and I appreciated that in the first few minutes we met. … He called me Lewis, and that decision endeared him to me even more; it was at once formal, my full name – We are gentleman here – and respectful. I was no baby Lewie. Lewis. I liked that."

Wooden went on to tell Alcindor what he expected from

Lew Alcindor, the towering New York freshman, takes his signature shot over the other players during a December 1964 game in Los Angeles, California.

his players. He then asked Alcindor if he had any questions. Alcindor answered that he liked the campus and that he really liked the Bruin basketball program.

"That's all very good," Wooden responded, "but I am impressed by your grades. You could do very well here as a student, whether you were an athlete or not. That is important."

As Abdul-Jabbar wrote: "Coach Wooden came through as a well-read, genuinely caring man. People would always tell me that they cared about me, but I felt Mr. Wooden really meant it. I came out of his office knowing I was going to UCLA."

Things didn't always go that smoothly. There was the time, for instance, when former assistant Denny Crum, who went on to great success as a head coach at the University of Louisville, recruited Bob McAdoo, who was one of the country's top prep players in 1969.

"I wrote him a letter and expressed an interest," Crum said, "and went back and tried to get his transcript to determine if he was eligible. They never would send it, [but] they kept saying they would. After two to three weeks of that Coach Wooden asked me how it was 'going with the McAdoo kid.' I said I haven't been able to get his transcript. Coach said to forget him and not recruit him.

"I told coach that McAdoo was the best player in the country. He said, 'Go spend your effort on someone who wants to come here. I'd rather coach players who want to come here. Even if they're not as good, they'll end up turning out just as good if they want to be here.' … That [was] Coach Wooden's attitude."

Wooden's focus, at least to his players, was on what they could control, what they needed to do to put themselves in the best possible position to do well.

Possibly the best example of that played out during the first day of practice each season when Wooden would stress to his players that their fingernails needed to stay trimmed and that their hair needed to be short. Then he

would demonstrate to his players the proper way to put their socks and shoes on. When done correctly, there were no kinks in the socks and no twists to the shoe laces.

"There is no way to describe the technique in words except to say that you really don't want to see Coach Wooden's bare feet," quipped Bill Walton, who took all four of his sons to Coach Wooden for the demonstration.

Subliminally, Wooden's sock and shoe practice showed the Bruins that they needed to take care of even the most minute details to be in a position to succeed.

But Wooden genuinely cared about his players. He made sure they were challenged on the court and in the classroom, by not allowing them to take only the easy courses. He wanted them to be as successful – if not more so – in the "real" world as in their years of playing for him. And he shot straight with them from the beginning.

He would tell them at the start of the season: "I don't like you all the same. You won't like me all the same. You won't like each other all the same. But I love you all the same."

"I'm going to treat you all the same and try to give you the treatment that you earn and deserve," he'd add. "You'll see that I'm not perfect, and sometimes I'll be wrong, but if I'm wrong too much, well, you don't have to worry about me. I'll be fired!"

Of course, he wasn't wrong very often. The wins and the championships were proof of that. Again, though, that wasn't necessarily his goal for his players.

"Some of the most successful coaches I know do not have a great winning percentage," Wooden said, "but they came closer to getting maximum potential out of the youngsters they have under their supervision.

"That determines your success; what you're able to get

Wooden introduces UCLA's new varsity basketball star, Lew Alcindor, at the Bruins' media day in Los Angeles, California.

from those you have under your supervision. I don't believe there's such a thing as an over-achiever, we're all underachievers to different degrees, but no one does more than they're capable of doing."

John Wooden's teams were successful because his players bought into his idea of winning basketball. They focused, over and over in practice, on the details. Wooden didn't necessarily have better players than other schools during the 1960 and '70s. In fact, during a few of those years, he didn't have as good of players as other schools. He just knew what it would take to get the most of out his players.

Wooden was not what one might consider today as a great game coach. He didn't make rah-rah speeches to his teams before they took the court. He rarely — sometimes but rarely — yelled at his players during the games. Rather, for the most part, he'd take the second seat down from the scorer's table and watch his team. After all, his players were prepared. That came from the grueling two-hour practices.

"I never considered myself anything but a teacher," he said. "I feel the games are the exams; you teach during the week."

During most of John Wooden's time in Westwood, that plan worked. A lot. Simply put: there's no denying UCLA's domination or its importance on the landscape of college basketball under John Wooden.

To put it into perspective, consider that out of the great coaches in the history of men's college basketball, not one has even half the number of championships that Wooden and his Bruins could boast. In fact, second behind Wooden's 10 is Adolph Rupp's four at Kentucky and Mike Krzyzewski's four at Duke.

Most of the time, the coaches who are fortunate enough to win multiple national titles will say that one isn't more special than the other. Although each of the Bruins's 10 national championships under Wooden could be highlighted as special — as they could for any coach because of

distinctive circumstances each time — the following are three of the more unique of the Final Fours, along with one loss that remains one of the most heartbreaking in the history of the UCLA program.

1964 — The One that Started It All

Coaches have a funny way of looking at things sometimes. Take Fred "Tex" Winter for instance.

Although Winter has been redefined during the past several decades as Phil Jackson's sage assistant with the Chicago Bulls and Los Angeles Lakers during those teams' title runs, Winter was an excellent college coach.

Gaining most of his success and popularity at Kansas State, Winter was the "father" of the widely-used triangle offense. He was also big on gamesmanship. When Wilt Chamberlain chose to play at rival Kansas, Winter strongly offered a few suggestions — such as raising the goals from 10 feet — to the NCAA rules committee in an attempt to stop Chamberlain from being so dominant.

So, when Wooden took the Bruins to the state of Kansas to play the Wildcats and the Jayhawks early in the 1964 season in the Sunflower Classic, Winter was outraged when someone at UCLA — allegedly athletic director J.D. Morgan — insisted that the Bruins wouldn't play in Kansas if they had to face the teams on their home courts. The other team in the classic was the University of Southern California, Winter's alma mater.

With UCLA as the headlining opponent, the idea was for each of the Kansas schools to play the Bruins on their home court and then the Trojans at the other school's home court. Instead, the schools acquiesced to UCLA's "request" and the Bruins played K-State in Lawrence on the KU cam-

Wooden is congratulated by President Fred Harrington of the University of Wisconsin after his team won the Milwaukee Classic tournament in Milwaukee, Wisconsin on December 20, 1964.

pus, and KU in Manhattan on the K-State campus. UCLA won both games, beating K-State by only three points.

UCLA and Kansas State happened to face each other again later that season at Kansas City's Municipal Auditorium – the same place where Wooden took Indiana State in 1948 – in the national tournament semifinals.

"In my mind there was a sense of payback when K-State and UCLA met in the NCAA tournament, because I wasn't too happy about the switching of opponents that took place in December," said Winter.

As the game moved along, it started to look as if it was going to be a repeat of 1962 for the Bruins – a loss in the semifinals. K-State led most of the game and took the Bruins out of their zone press, a Wooden staple during his teams' championship runs.

But the momentum began to shift in favor of the under-sized Bruins, a team without a starter taller than 6-foot-5.

"We thought we had UCLA beat," said K-State's 6-6 guard Willie Murrell, who scored a game-high 29 points. "We led the whole game, including by five points late, but we missed our shots at the end. They somehow stopped our shooting."

The Bruins went on to win the game, 90-84, behind Keith Erickson's 28 points and Hazzard's 19. UCLA was headed to its first national championship game.

A funny side note. One legend with K-State fans is that the Bruins started taking control of the game because of the UCLA cheerleaders. For some reason, they didn't show up at the game until the final seven or eight minutes, with the Wildcats still up by about five points. Allegedly, a K-State player missed a victory-sealing layup when the cheerleaders entered Municipal. That didn't go completely unnoticed for the Bruins, though.

"At that point our cheerleaders, delayed by travel difficulties, rushed into the arena and brought some much-needed moral support," Erickson wrote in the book "Champions Again!" "We promptly ran off 11 points in

a row and held off K-State."

The next night, the Bruins cruised past Duke, 98-83, thanks largely to a 16-0 run late in the first half that gave UCLA a 43-30 advantage, and by the play of Kenny Washington. Coming off the bench, Washington ignited the Bruins with 26 points. John Wooden had his first national title with a perfect 30-0 record.

In a story that illustrates the type of person John Wooden was, as happy as he should've been that his team won, he had a disappointed feeling. One of his seniors and main players throughout the season, Fred Slaughter, the 6-5 player who grew up in nearby Topeka and had turned down scholarship offers from Kansas and Kansas State, had a bad game against Duke. So bad, in fact, that Wooden pulled Slaughter and played Doug McIntosh most of the game.

As Wooden walked toward the team locker room, his "spirits dragged" because of how he thought Slaughter, who happened to be UCLA's student-body president, must have felt. Of course, when he opened the locker room door, Slaughter was the first person he saw.

Immediately, Slaughter let Wooden know that although he was disappointed in his performance, he understood that for the team's sake Wooden had to play McIntosh.

"You know, there are a lot of peaks and valleys in every coach's life," Wooden wrote in "They Call Me Coach." "But this was the peak – the ultimate. We had won our first, my first, NCAA title … But my concern for Fred had damaged all of that until this moment. Now I felt really great!"

In spite of losing three main seniors from that team, the Bruins repeated as champions in 1965 when they beat Michigan in the championship. But the 1964 title was, well, the first.

Lew Alcindor cuts down the net after leading the Bruins to a 78-55 victory over North Carolina for their second straight NCAA Championship.

"That first championship also sparked a chain of events which helped us win those nine additional championships," said Wooden. "Recruiting after that 1964 national championship was tremendous. … We also got a new place to play after winning those first championships which helped tremendously. Lew Alcindor would never have come to UCLA had it not been for the new Pauley Pavilion, nor would he have come had we not won in 1964 and 1965. Those years attracted his attention."

Tex Winter's take?

"I've often wondered if Johnny Wooden hadn't won that if they would've won all those championships," he said. "They probably would've won, but who knows. The next one might have been more difficult for them. I guess you can say that beating us started their streak."

Yes, coaches have a funny way of seeing things.

1968 — Boosting College Basketball in the National Spotlight

Remember the idea of Wooden having his team only focus on their game plan during practice, instead of developing a strategy for their upcoming opponent? Well, there was at least one time when that changed.

Heading into the '68 semifinal game against Houston, Wooden and his players felt – rather, they knew – they were better than the Cougars. Reading that now it might not seem like such a big deal.

The short rivalry began at the end of the 1967 season. With big man Elvin Hayes, then a junior, many people felt that Houston would beat UCLA in the national semifinals, especially considering Wooden started four sophomores – including Lew Alcindor – and one junior. Instead, the Bruins won that game easily and, eventually, the national title.

However, during the regular season, on January 20, 1968, ranked Nos. 1 and 2, UCLA and Houston met at the Astrodome in Houston, in the first nationally televised regular-season college basketball game – in prime time, no less. That wasn't the only first.

It was the first in a domed stadium, which is commonplace for today's Final Fours. It was the first time a crowd of more than 50,000 (52,693) watched a game in person. And, with an injured Alcindor, who'd been scratched in his left eye a few days earlier, and Hayes scoring 39 points and grabbing 15 rebounds, it was the first time UCLA had lost in 47 games. The Cougars won 71-69.

Instead of being mad about the loss or concerned about the end of the winning streak or anything else, Wooden was very calm in the locker room afterwards. After all, he felt his players did their best.

"It's not the end of the world," he told the Bruins, almost with a smile on his face. "We'll do better next time."

Even in the years after the loss, Wooden never made excuses for UCLA losing that game. Although he did feel relatively confident that they'd do better if they faced the Cougars again.

"Playing in front of a big crowd like that was not intimidating for us," Wooden said. "As far as being an emotional game, it wasn't for me or for my team, because it was a non-conference game. Since teams had to win their conference to be in the NCAA tournament, that was always our aim at the beginning of the year. … We didn't place as much emphasis on the games with teams outside of our conference back then."

"I felt that if we played them again," Wooden added, "with Alcindor healthy, that we'd do very, very well."

Wooden calls for timeout in the waning seconds of a game against the University of Houston in the Astrodome in Houston, Texas on January 20, 1968. Wooden made the call in an effort to set up a play which he hoped might put his Bruins ahead. Seconds later Houston forward Elvin Hayes was awarded two free throws which he made to win the game for Houston, 71-69.

Besides that knowledge or confidence or whatever you want to call UCLA's attitude toward Houston, that was simply it. To a man, there wasn't a revenge factor.

As fate would have it, UCLA and Houston met again that year, in the NCAA tournament semifinals. With or without Alcindor at full strength, there was no denying the ability of Elvin Hayes. He was a big, dominating force under the basket, which he proved to the Bruins in that first meeting in 1968. So, even with a healthy Alcindor, Wooden didn't take any chances. He unveiled a slightly different defensive scheme against the Cougars: a diamond-and-one.

Wooden had Lynn Shackelford, who wasn't one of the Bruins' best defensive players, shadow Hayes. Alcindor stayed under the basket to defend it. The other three Bruins stretched across the court in a match-up zone.

"The one time I ever saw coach Wooden change his game plan was for Elvin Hayes," said Lucius Allen, one of the guards on that UCLA squad. "(Houston) wasn't expecting that and the rest is history."

That history included a Bruin route, 101-69. Lew Alcindor, Lucius Allen and Mike Lynn led UCLA with 19 points apiece. The championship wasn't much of a contest, either, as the Bruins captured their fourth title with a 78-55 win over North Carolina.

"Despite what a lot of people think, I don't agree with the idea that Lew Alcindor was the big difference in the outcome of the two games (with the Cougars)," said Houston coach Guy Lewis. "I think the UCLA coaching staff was the difference. The Bruin staff figured out something before the 1968 semifinal game that no other coaching staff had exposed all season — that we had only one shooter on the team, even though we led the nation in scoring for two years.

"Their coaching staff ran a different defense in the semifinals that effectively took Elvin out of his game and it killed us."

"Coach had an ace up his sleeve," Allen said. "We were the better team anyway, but Coach surprised them."

Showing great wisdom as well as a love and respect for all of his players, Wooden would never reveal directly which team of his 10 that won the championship he felt was the best. That's like asking a parent which child he favors. Besides, four of the 10 teams went undefeated, three had just one loss, and then there was his final one. But the 1967-68 club certainly held a special place with Coach.

"I will say that the 1968 squad would be more difficult to play against than most of the other teams I had at UCLA," Wooden said. "That team would pose more problems than the others because they had all of the ingredients."

Incidentally, that Houston game was the first time Wooden's UCLA teams used a diamond-and-one defense. It also was the last.

1973 — Completing the Back-to-Back, Undefeated Championship String

It seemed nearly impossible — in spite of UCLA's championship run, which stood at six straight — that a team could be so dominating. Or, maybe because it was a Wooden-coached team, it did seem possible. But, heading into the 1973 national championship game against Memphis State, after knocking off Indiana in the semifinals, the Bruins had won 74 consecutive games. Nearly unfathomable today.

And it was dominating with a lanky junior from San Diego named Bill Walton.

As with many boys who could play basketball from Southern California by that time, UCLA was the dream

Wooden smiles while holding the game ball as he leads his players off the floor after beating Notre Dame for a record 61st win in South Bend, Indiana on January 27, 1973.

Bill Walton encourages his teammates from the bench during the first half of the game between UCLA and North Carolina State on December 15, 1973.

school. That held true for Bill Walton, whose older brother Bruce was on the Bruin football team when Bill was a high school basketball star.

Wooden and assistant coach Denny Crum were urged to take a look at Walton. If there was one aspect of coaching that Wooden never liked it was recruiting. However, Crum went down to San Diego one night to see how good this Walton kid was.

The next morning he reported to Wooden: "I think he's the best high school player I've ever seen."

Wooden jumped out of his chair, closed the door and said, "Don't ever make that kind of statement where anybody can hear you. It will make you look like an idiot. Plus, San Diego has never even had a Division I player, let alone the best player you've ever seen."

Crum wrote in "CBS Sports Presents: Stories from the Final Four": "I told (Wooden), 'Even if you don't believe that this could be the best high school basketball player I've ever seen, for us to get this kid you need to come watch him play and show a little interest.'

"We took the 20-minute flight to San Diego during the week to see Bill play. … When we got to our seats, I just let him watch the game in peace. I didn't say anything to him.

"On our way back to the airport after the game I asked Coach what he thought about Walton. Wooden said, 'Well, he is pretty good, isn't he.' Coach Wooden didn't like to praise individuals, he liked to talk about the team, so when he made that comment, it meant that he liked Walton a lot. Luckily for us, the feeling was mutual from Walton."

Luckily, indeed. Walton, whom many consider to be the best player in the history of college basketball, bordered on unstoppable.

When Walton first stepped onto the UCLA campus with his long red hair, he looked like he should be carrying a surf board, not a basketball. Also, imagine the looks he got when riding around campus on his 10-speed bike.

Throughout his career, with his outspoken social and political views, both of which were a little more liberal than his coach's, Walton clashed often with Wooden. He wasn't afraid to challenge him. But he never wanted to disappoint Wooden.

Wooden, as a rule, wouldn't allow his players to have long hair or any facial hair. He believed in that so much that not only did he stress that verbally to his players, but it also was in the letter he sent to his squad each season.

On the first day of practice one season, Walton couldn't wait to see his coach at practice. After all, Walton wanted to show off his long hair and beard.

Wooden took one look at Walton, pointed to Walton's hair and said: "What's this? That's unacceptable. You can't practice today, Bill."

Walton, who would become a three-time Player of the Year award winner, tried to flex his rebellious muscle and tell Wooden that he could wear his hair any way he wanted. And that Wooden didn't have the "right" to tell him that he couldn't have long hair.

"You're correct, Bill, I don't have that right. I just have the right to determine who's going to play," Wooden said. Then he calmly added, "We're going to miss you.

"In about 15 minutes I'm not going to have you unless you go upstairs and get it taken care of right away."

Walton gave Wooden a dumbfounded look.

"Fourteen minutes," Wooden said sternly.

Walton bolted for the door, hopped on his bike and pedaled as fast as he could to the barbershop in Westwood.

"Cut it all off. And give me a plastic razor and a glass of water," he said.

In a flash, the cleaner-looking Walton raced back to

Bill Walton goes up to block a shot by Ohio's Denny Rush during the first half of their game at Pauley Pavilion in Los Angeles on December 21, 1973.

Pauley Pavilion on his bike and sneaked in, five minutes late to practice – hoping Wooden wouldn't notice.

Even though Walton dominated most of his opponents while at UCLA, no other game was quite like the 1973 national championship contest against Memphis State.

Walton delivered one of the best single-game performances ever known in a Final Four. He scored 44 points and shot 21-for-22 from the field. The one shot he missed, on a lob pass, rolled out. (But he got his own rebound and scored.) It didn't hurt that the Bruins had Greg Lee, who accounted for 14 assists, an NCAA title-game record.

The Bruins crushed a good Tiger team, 87-66. In the process, besides upping their winning streak to 75 games, UCLA became the first and only team to go undefeated in consecutive seasons.

"The Memphis State game was not about me as an individual, even though I get far too much credit for it," Walton said. "The game was about UCLA basketball and the dreams of John Wooden coming together. We wanted to win for Coach Wooden. I could never imagine playing for anyone in college other than him.

"Coach challenged each of us to play our perfect game, and to create an environment where it was our style of game being played. He was an unbelievable teacher in preparing us mentally, spiritually and physically. When game time came, we felt that we were invincible and could do anything we wanted.

And that night against Memphis State, they pretty much did.

1974 — The Heartbreaking Loss

Bill Walton, who had considered jumping to the NBA after his junior year on the hardship rule, came back for one last run. On a cold March evening in 1974, in Greensboro, North Carolina, he might've regretted that decision.

The 1973-74 season was cruising along as well as the Bruins and their coach could've hoped. They were an experienced team. And they didn't have many close games. The only problem, if you want to call it that, was that they kept winning. And winning. And winning. It had been so long since they'd lost, in fact, that Wooden was growing slightly concerned about the pressure and whether they were trying to win or trying not to lose.

By mid-January, their winning streak, which began on January 23, 1971, was up to a remarkable 88 games. That is until they faced Notre Dame on January 19 in South Bend, Indiana.

Behind a 12-0 run in the final few minutes of the game, the Irish ended UCLA's streak, 71-70. Incidentally, the last team to beat the Bruins before "the streak?" Notre Dame. At South Bend.

But Wooden had his team back on track quickly. The Bruins, with any pressure they might've felt with "the streak" gone, kept their focus on another national championship.

As expected, they reached the Final Four once again, along with Kansas, Marquette, and their semifinal opponent, North Carolina State.

In spite of beating the Wolfpack by 18 early in the season in St. Louis, N.C. State posed a threat to the Bruins. At least the teams believed so. The Wolfpack boasted big players inside with 7-foot-4 Tom Burleson, quick point guard Monte Towe, future Major League pitcher Tim Stoddard as a bruiser at one forward, and the athletic David Thompson at the other forward.

The game was billed as Walton vs. Thompson, but it turned out to be a total team effort on both ends. Sure, Walton and Thompson lived up to their billing. Walton finished the game with 29 points and 14 rebounds, while

Bill Walton and Wooden dejectedly leave the floor after Notre Dame ended the All-American's winning streak at 142 games in high school and with the Bruins on January 19, 1974.

Thompson scored 28 with 10 boards.

Uncharacteristic of Wooden's teams, the Bruins blew two sizeable late leads. During the second half, UCLA was ahead comfortably by 11 points. The Wolfpack came back. Then, in the second overtime, the Bruins were up by seven. Again, though, UCLA squandered the lead.

In the end, though, North Carolina State won 80-77 in double-overtime.

"He was the master of preparation," Walton said of Wooden. "He was all about us. We never talked about the other team in the four years I was at UCLA. Only twice did he mention other players. In my freshman year, he talked about (Notre Dame's) Austin Carr. In my senior year, he talked about David Thompson.

"We lost both those games."

Since that time, much has been made about Walton leading the chorus of Bruins in saying they weren't going to play Kansas in the consolation game. It wasn't a disrespect to the Jayhawks as much as the Bruins' belief that they were there to play for only the championship.

Wooden, however, wouldn't have any of that. He insisted that his team, even the senior Walton, play for third place. UCLA won easily, 78-61. But there was no consolation for the Bruins.

As Walton said in 1999: "Coach Wooden told us every day, 'Don't ever beat yourself. Do your best so that you can consider yourself a success. If you beat yourself, or cheat yourself, it's the worst kind of defeat you'll ever suffer and you'll never get over it.'

"He was right about beating ourselves. He was right about everything. We certainly have never gotten over that embarrassing defeat of March 23, 1974. With an 11-point lead in the second half, then with a seven-point lead

(above) Wooden listens to Greg Lee during a timeout in a game against Iowa in Chicago, Illinois in 1974. (opposite) Bill Walton goes high to grab the rebound in the first half against USC on March 9, 1974.

and the ball in the closing minutes of the second overtime, it was a game that should have been ours. I have been kicking myself ever since. That day I was a disgrace to the sport of basketball."

It wasn't much easier for Wooden. He often said that he thought about only two losses regularly: the Indiana State Championship game against Muncie Central during Wooden's senior year of 1928, and the North Carolina State match.

Wooden said: "Of all the losses I ever had at UCLA that was the most devastating."

Possibly the most devastating for UCLA would come a year later. ●

UCLA's Andre McCarter starts a pass to teammate Pete Tregovich (right, No. 25) in a game against Davidson on January 4, 1975 in Los Angeles, California.

The End of an Era

Going through the 1975 season and then the NCAA tournament, no one could've expected what was about to happen. Oh, the tournament always has some unexpected storylines. But no one could've seen this coming for UCLA – not the fans, not the players, not even John Wooden himself.

For all intents and purposes, the 1975 Bruins were a team, at the time, of no-names. Not to take anything away from the likes of Dave Meyers, Richard Washington, Marques Johnson and Pete Trgovich, but they weren't Greg Lee, Keith Wilkes and Bill Walton, three of the players gone from the previous year's team. At least not at the time. Meyers was the only returning starter from the 1974 Bruin team that was stunned by in the semifinals by North Carolina State.

As the Bruins had done the previous season, they lost only two games during the 1974-75 Pacific-8 schedule, and went into the NCAA tournament with a 23-3 record.

The tournament itself was anything but a cakewalk for Wooden and his no-name players. It took overtime for UCLA to get past Michigan in the opening round. Then the Bruins beat Montana by three points in their second-round game, before cruising past Arizona State for a trip to the Final Four at the San Diego Arena.

Up next for the Bruins was a meeting with Louisville, coached by one of Wooden's former players and assistant coaches, Denny Crum.

The two teams played a fantastic game. It's one of the few games, in fact, that Wooden often said was nearly perfect. (To Wooden, of course, there was never a perfect game.) After playing to a 65-65 tie at the end of regulation, the Bruins went on to win the contest in dramatic fashion with sophomore Richard Washington hitting a 10-foot jumper with less than 5 seconds remaining in overtime. Louisville's Allen Murphy threw up a desperation shot at the buzzer that missed.

UCLA was headed to its 10th national championship game. The Bruins had yet to lose in a NCAA title game under Wooden.

Just how good was the UCLA-Louisville contest? In his personal notes for practice the next day, Wooden wrote: "When you consider the play of each time [team], I felt this was the finest NCAA tournament game in which I had ever had a team involved."

Wooden, however, didn't feel quite right in the seconds after the semifinal game. He had suffered a mild heart attack a couple years earlier, but he wasn't feeling badly. But after the Louisville contest, Wooden wasn't as excited as he should've been. As he fought through the pandemonium of the euphoric crowd and headed toward the press conference after quickly hugging Crum, Wooden was drained.

"I'm really wrung out," he thought to himself.

Then, it hit him.

"Gee," he thought, "if I'm feeling like this after such a

Wooden holds his head during the final minutes of the NCAA semifinal against Louisville on March 29, 1975.

Coach John Wooden

beautiful game, maybe it's time to get out."

So, instead of talking with reporters and dropping the word of his retirement, Wooden did the only thing that was right for him. He walked to the Bruin locker room to tell his players. After all, his mind was made up. There was no sense in delaying the inevitable.

Wooden went inside to the wild celebration that only college-aged kids can display, stood on a chair in the middle of the room and looked around at these no-name players – a group that was on the verge of doing what no one outside Southern California thought they could do – as he waited for them to quiet down. Once they did, he mentioned their upcoming game on Monday with

(above) Wooden, who won 10 national titles in 27 years as head coach, walks with his wife, Nell, as they pass between former UCLA players in a birthday salute to the retiring coach. (opposite) Wooden wears a basketball net around his neck after his team won the 1975 NCAA basketball championship over Kentucky.

Kentucky before subtly delivering his news.

"I don't know how we will do, but I think we will do OK. I think we have enough quickness," he said. "But I want you to know, regardless of how it comes out, I never had a group that gave me less trouble. You gave me no trouble on or off the court all year and I'm extremely

proud of you. That's a very nice thing to be able to say about the last team I'll ever teach."

Forget the cliché about hearing a pin drop. You probably could've heard a feather drop. Everyone was stunned.

Throughout the rest of his life Wooden asserted – and never strayed from the fact – that he did not know before that moment that he was going to retire that night, or even that season. It wasn't until walking across the court after the Louisville game. He often said that if anyone had asked him before that moment about his future, he would've said that he'd be around for another two or three years. Instead, at the age of 64, three years from California's mandatory retirement age at the time, he was going to coach the Bruins in one last game. Appropriately, the national championship.

Before preparing for Monday's game, though, Wooden had to face the media with the news of his retirement. Much like the way he told his players, he immediately and calmly announced it to the reporters.

"I'm asking Athletic Director J.D. Morgan to relieve me of my duties as head coach of UCLA at the conclusion of this tournament," he said.

That was that. Of course, hours after the press conference, a stunned Morgan tried to get Wooden to change his mind. It was no use. As Wooden had displayed throughout his life and his career, once he made a decision, he stuck to it.

Wooden said years later: "I never faulted the decision I made that evening. It was right, and it was timely."

The only other thing left for Wooden and the 1974-75 Bruins was to prepare for Monday's championship game against Kentucky.

Even though Wooden never believed in artificial or external motivation, this game was going to be a little different for the players. How could it not be? What better way to send Wooden out than with his 10th national championship?

"We were at the right emotional level," Trgovich said.

"We were ready to win for The Man, not emotionally yelling and screaming, but feeling it inside. I knew we were ready for the big one."

Behind Richard Washington's 28 points and 12 rebounds, and Dave Meyers's 24 points and 11 rebounds – not to mention Wooden using only Ralph Drollinger off the bench – the Bruins held off the Wildcats down the stretch and won, 92-85.

Amid the post-game celebration, a fan helped Wooden realize that he made the right decision.

Shortly before the awards presentation, one of UCLA's top boosters went up to Wooden, shook his hand excitedly and yelled in his ear: "It was a great victory, John … after you let us down last year."

UCLA's victory was a fitting swan song for Wooden, and, indeed, great timing for the NCAA.

UCLA fans weren't the only ones who expected the Bruins to win each year. Considering Texas Western (now the University of Texas-El Paso) in 1966 and North Carolina State in 1974 were the only two teams to win the championship since UCLA's first one in 1964, college basketball fans were beginning to lose interest in the tournament. There was a thought that there wasn't a reason to pay attention because nobody could beat UCLA.

Of course, looking back, UCLA's tournament domination under John Wooden came at the perfect time. The NCAA needed a team to pique everyone's interest to advance the tournament on a national scale. Wooden and his Bruins did just that. They were dominating, likeable and fun to watch. And – with all due respect to the players – it was all because of one man. ●

A stoic Wooden applauds as members of his team are introduced before the NCAA national championship game against Kentucky in San Diego, California on March 31, 1975.

Wooden works as a game announcer with Merle Harmon as UCLA won its NCAA Western Regional game against Pepperdine in Los Angeles, California on March 18, 1976.

Wooden's Words of Wisdom

Bill Walton spouts the homespun phrases off as if he's reciting his favorite Grateful Dead songs. Or his address. That's because the Bruins all heard John Wooden's maxims every day in practice. Constantly.

"We thought, 'This is kind of weird. What's this silly old man talking about?'" said Walton.

Wooden was passing along his words of wisdom — the maxims, quotes, poems — that were going to help prepare his team.

"Failing to prepare is preparing to fail. Do your best so you can consider yourself a success. We thought he was absolutely crazy," Walton added, "but at the time we were winning all of our games. It wasn't until we started losing that we realized the lessons and messages that he was giving us were absolutely the right ones."

Although most of the following can be found in nearly every book or article about Wooden, these are many of the ideas that shaped him and — because of him — those around him. Unless otherwise noted, most of these are attributed to Wooden.

"Try your hardest, make the effort, do your best."
— Wooden stressed this to his players. Although it's not a direct quote from his dad Joshua, John Wooden says the philosophy came from his dad's teachings.

"At God's footstool to confess,
"A poor soul knelt and bowed his head.
"I failed," he cried. The master said,

"Thou didst thy best. That is success."
— The source of this poem is unknown, but Joshua Wooden read this to his sons often, and John Wooden referred to it often to help illustrate success and the importance of giving one's all.

"Don't lie.
"Don't cheat.
"Don't steal."
And
"Don't whine.
"Don't complain.
"Don't make excuses."
— Joshua Wooden's "Two Sets of Three," given to John when he was in grade school. He often said it was a formula for success.

"Success is peace of mind that is a direct result of self-satisfaction in knowing you did your best to become the best that you are capable of becoming."
— John Wooden's definition of success, which helped him build the Pyramid of Success

"Things work out for the best for those who make the best of the way things work out."

"When you're through learning, you're through."

Wooden scowls during the Bruins 25th win in March 3, 1964 which put them within one game of a perfect regular season.

"If I were prosecuted for my religion, I truly hope there would be enough evidence to convict."

"Passion is momentary; love is enduring."
"Be more concerned with your character than your reputation."

"O Lord, if I seem to lose my faith in Thee, do not Thou lose Thy faith in me."

"Do not mistake activity for achievement."

"There is no substitute for work."

"Who can ask more of a man
than giving all within his span?
Giving all, it seems to me,
is not so far from victory."
– *George Moriarty, "The Road Ahead of the Road Behind"*

"You must earn the right to be confident."

"If you keep too busy learning the tricks of the trade, you may never learn the trade."

"It is amazing how much we can accomplish when no one cares who gets the credit."

"Goals achieved with little effort are seldom appreciated and give no personal satisfaction."

"I am just a common man who is true to his beliefs."

"Do not let what you cannot do interfere with what you can do."

"You never fail if you know in your heart that you did the best of which you are capable."

"There is nothing stronger than gentleness."
– *Abraham Lincoln*
"The greatest word in the dictionary is love."

"Be quick but don't hurry."

"Ability may get you to the top, but it takes character to keep you there."

"You are the only one who knows whether you have won."

"Motivation must come from the belief that ultimate success lies in giving your personal best."

"The main ingredient of stardom is the rest of the team."

Six Ways to Bring Out the Best in People
1. Keep courtesy and consideration for others foremost in your mind, at home and away.
2. Try to have fun without trying to be funny.
3. While you can't control what happens to you, you can control how you react. Make good manners an automatic reaction.
4. Seek individual opportunities to offer a genuine compliment.
5. Remember that sincerity, optimism, and enthusiasm are more welcome than sarcasm, pessimism, and laziness.
6. Laugh with others, never at them.

Wooden reacts to a questionable call from officials during a Bruins game.

Coach John Wooden

"It's what you learn after you know it all that counts."

"Young people need models, not critics."

"Be slow to criticize and quick to commend."

"Failure to act is often the biggest failure of all."

"The person you are is the person your child will become."

"A man may make mistakes, but he isn't a failure until he starts blaming someone else."

"Success is never final. Failure is never fatal. It's courage that counts."
— *Winston Churchill*

"Little things done well is probably the greatest secret to success."

"Whatever you do in life, surround yourself with smart people who'll argue with you."

"Happiness begins when selfishness ends."

"Talent is God-given; be humble.
Fame is man-given; be thankful.
Conceit is self-given; be careful."

"Failing to prepare is preparing to fail."

"Time spent getting even would be better spent getting ahead."

"Respect every opponent, but fear none."

"Discipline yourself and others won't have to."

"The true athlete should have character but not be a character."

"A careful man I want to be,
A little fellow follows me;
I do not dare to go astray,
For fear he'll go the self-same way."

"Four things a man must do
If he would make his life more true:
To think without confusion clearly,
To love his fellow man sincerely,
To act from honest motives purely,
To trust in God and Heaven securely."
— *Rev. Henry Van Dyke*

Joshua Wooden's Seven-Point Creed
1. Be true to yourself.
2. Help others.
3. Make each day your masterpiece.
4. Drink deeply from good books – especially the Bible.
5. Make friendship a fine art.
6. Build shelter against a rainy day (faith in God).
7. Pray for guidance and counsel and give thanks for your blessings each day. ●

Wooden poses for a picture after a news conference in December 2005, about the upcoming Wooden Classic basketball tournament.

W

WOODEN

®

ssic

Boston College's Steve Hailey, right, dribbles the ball as UCLA's Jordan Farmar guards him during the first half at the 11th Annual John R. Wooden Classic in December 2004, in Anaheim, California.

Leaving a Legacy

There should be a rule at every level of sports. Suspend play for two years after a "legendary" coach retires. It would make life easier for the "transition coach," the coach who is destined for failure if for no reason besides the fact he's following a legend.

As the story goes, Joe B. Hall, who succeeded Adolph Rupp at Kentucky, said in 1975 that UCLA should hire him as Wooden's replacement. "Why ruin two lives?" Hall quipped, referring to the man who'd eventually succeed Wooden.

Life certainly hasn't been easy for UCLA, or its coaches, since John Wooden retired in 1975. Going from a school with an average basketball program before Wooden to the national power it became under him gave Bruin fans incredible expectations. Considering Wooden's teams' unparalleled accomplishments, the expectations were unfair for any successor.

In Wooden's mind, though, the job at UCLA was always one of the best in the country. He once acknowledged that it should've been difficult for his replacement. But in his own humble way, he didn't see the job as being tough for any of the eight men who have coached the Bruins since then.

"(Coaching at UCLA) isn't a hard thing," he said. "It's the easiest place in the world. There's more material here, they have the best place to play on, and good coaching. … (Coaches at UCLA) don't need my blessing. They have it, whoever it is."

Of course, as anyone knows, it's never easy following a legend. Just ask Gene Bartow, Wooden's immediate replacement, who went 52-9, won two conference championships and reached the Final Four. He left, feeling the pressure in Westwood, to start the program at Alabama-Birmingham.

UCLA athletic director J.D. Morgan had a host of possibilities. His list included former UCLA player and Wooden assistant Denny Crum, who was at Louisville, and North Carolina's Dean Smith.

Crum said: "When your alma mater calls, it's not an easy thing to say no." But, Crum did just that. As did Smith.

UCLA hired Gary Cunningham, who also was an assistant for Wooden – and one of Wooden's preferences as his original replacement. Cunningham went 50-8 in his two seasons and won two conference titles. And then stepped down.

Then came Larry Brown. And Larry Farmer. And Walt Hazzard.

By the end of Hazzard's three seasons, UCLA had gone through five head coaches in 13 years.

It didn't look as if anyone could live up to the mystique created by Wooden. Finally, in 1995, under Jim Harrick, the Bruins won the national championship. In a funny way, however, no matter how many trips the Bruins make to the Final Four, as they did in 2006 and 2007

Wooden talks with members of Saint Mary's after they defeated San Diego State in their basketball game at the John R. Wooden Classic in December 2007.

under Ben Howland, or how many national championships the Bruins win, in the foreseeable future many fans will compare the coach to John Wooden.

"It is a very difficult job at UCLA," said Pete Newell, one of Wooden's long-time coaching friends and rivals who won the national championship at Cal in 1959. "You are not allowed to learn from your mistakes at UCLA like you could at other places. No one can change the atmosphere there. I think you will always be fighting the shadows."

Another Dark Cloud

John Wooden's 10 national championships in 12 seasons are in stone. If there is to be a blemish on his record, however, it would be the name Sam Gilbert.

In the early years following Wooden's retirement, questions arose about Gilbert, who was a pudgy, balding, jovial Los Angeles contractor and UCLA booster. He had a look that would've allowed him to fit easily in the Chicago and New York mob scene of the 1920s and '30s.

Wooden admitted over time that he broke NCAA rules by letting players eat at his house during school breaks. He bailed Bill Walton out of jail one time after Walton was involved in one of his many protests. Wooden also helped pay the rent of another player, who had a child.

But those paled in comparison to Gilbert, who, beginning somewhere around the late-1960s, started giving the Bruin players whatever they wanted – money, expensive clothes, advice – and had them at his house regularly.

"The way Sam explained it to me, it was within the rules," Lucius Allen said in the 2007 documentary "The UCLA Dynasty." Allen paused and then added, "But it wasn't."

Many players believe that Wooden knew about Gilbert's involvement to an extent, but he didn't get involved.

"He worried me," Wooden added in the documentary. "I was worried all the time. I was afraid that he was going to do something illegal to the players."

In 1981, UCLA was placed on probation for two years because of activities of an unidentified booster after 1975. Then, in 1982, the NCAA told UCLA to ban Gilbert from having contact with the program. Sam Gilbert died in 1987.

Nell

Life wasn't easy for John Wooden, either, during the first decade after he retired in 1975. The biggest curve was with his dear Nellie.

Since that summer day in 1926 at the Martinsville carnival, John Wooden was smitten with Nell. And what a pair they were. When Nell Riley played the cornet in the Martinsville High band, and Johnny Wooden was a sophomore getting ready to play for the Artisians, he found her and winked. She gave him the "OK" sign with her hand. That ritual continued throughout his playing career. Then, as a coach, he'd find Nell in the crowd and wave his rolled up program at her.

Where he was shy and reserved, she was energetic and outgoing. When they'd be at a gathering where John might not remember names, she'd whisper a person's name in his ear as they approached.

They adored each other. Many players will tell you today that watching John and Nell together was an impressionable blessing.

In 1984, Nell went into a coma after surgery. John stayed at her bedside, day and night, holding her hand, talking to her, praying for her. Ninety days later, Nell came out of the coma. She went back to the hospital on Christmas Eve of that year.

Johnny Wooden's "sweetheart of 60 years," Nell, passed away on March 21, 1985.

Wooden and his wife, Nell, look over a photo album at their home in Santa Monica, California in March 1970. For 37 years the couple had a ritual before every game in which they exchanged "OK" signs.

"If you dropped a small pebble into the deepest part of the ocean on the darkest night of the year – that was me without Nell," Wooden wrote in "My Personal Best."

From that point until the end of his life, Wooden kept everything in their condo in Encino just the way it had been when she was living. He slept on his side of the bed and on top of the covers. When he sent birthday cards to friends and family members, he signed both of their names.

And, on the 21st of every month, Wooden would sit down and write a love letter to Nell. He would put it in an envelope and add it to the stack of notes that he'd written on the 21st of every other month and carefully tied together with a ribbon.

"I was never preoccupied with dying," Wooden added in "My Personal Best." "But perhaps like most people, I feared it. Losing Nell has cured me of any fear of death because I believe that when I'm called, when the Good Lord beckons according to his plan, I will go to heaven and be with her. Knowing this gives me peace."

His Legacy

During the last few years of his life, John Wooden received deserving high local, state and national honors.

On October 14, 2006, the day Wooden turned 96, the Reseda, California branch of the Post Office changed its name to the Coach John Wooden Post Office.

That came on the heels of a ceremony six months earlier during which Wooden received the 2005 Sachem, which is the highest honor given by the state of Indiana. The award is given by the governor to one Indiana native annually.

The highest honor of all, though, came a few years earlier. On July 23, 2003, President George W. Bush presented Wooden with the Presidential Medal of Freedom, the highest honor for an American citizen.

Without Wooden's knowledge, several of his former players and admirers had been sending letters to the White House for years, trying to get him noticed for the award.

Then, one day, he received a FedEx package.

"(He) ripped it open and found a letter from President Bush," Steve Bisheff described in his book, "John Wooden: An American Treasure." "When asked what it was, the coach's eyes filled with tears. 'I'm just not worthy,' he said. The reaction of everyone who knew him was: If he's not worthy, then who is?"

There was a poem several years ago called "The Dash," about how the important thing for a person is how he lived his life from birth until death – basically, the "dash" mark between those two years.

In basketball, there never can be any denying or questioning his accomplishments as a player or as a coach.

On and off the court, although he wasn't perfect, John Wooden gave everyone around him – and anyone else who would pay attention to his teachings and sayings – a wonderful example of how to make that dash matter. He definitely made it count.

"(Coach Wooden) figured out how to take the two things that he valued most, family and basketball, to do his life's work and the Lord's work," said Kareem Abdul-Jabbar. "That's not always easy, but he pulled it off. There aren't a whole lot of people who can say that."

"We love Coach Wooden," Bill Walton said. "He really did give us everything. He taught us how to learn, taught us how to think, taught us how to dream, taught us how to be part of a team. He never told us the answers. He just told us how to get there."

Others on Wooden

"I have told people quite often that every UCLA basketball player who spent time under Coach Wooden's

Kevin Love shows the John R. Wooden Classic trophy to John Wooden after UCLA defeated Davidson at the John R. Wooden Classic basketball tournament in December 2007.

tutelage received more than improved skills. He received a way of thinking about solving problems and overcoming obstacles. If you paid attention and believed in what he said, you not only became a better basketball player, you also became a more competent person. He was as much a philosopher as a coach, and he was equally proficient at both activities. My basketball skills I lost long ago, but the life principles he left with me are more valuable today than they were when I first heard them."

— Doug McIntosh, UCLA 1964-66, who went on to become a minister in the Atlanta area.

"Few people in any walk of life have combined such overwhelming success with such unshakeable integrity. The America that produced John Wooden is gone. The principles which guided his life and career endure."

— Sportscaster Bob Costas

"You know, I realize there have been some great coaches in college basketball. But I don't think any other coach affected his ballplayers the way Johnny Wooden affected his ballplayers. I don't mean just at the time. I mean for the rest of their lives. He didn't just make you a better player. He made you a better person."

— Sidney Wicks, UCLA 1969-71, who was known to get into it with Wooden from time to time.

"There has never been a finer coach in American sports than John Wooden. Nor a finer man."

— Columnist Rick Reilly

"There has never been another coach like Wooden, quiet as an April snow and square as a game of checkers; loyal to one woman, one school, one way; walking around campus in his sensible shoes and Jimmy Stewart morals."

— Rick Reilly

"Before practice, he'd often be standing there as we walked on to the court: 'How's your mother, David? Have you called her?' 'You over that cold, Jim?' 'How's the math class coming?' He knew us as people. You could tell he cared. And you could tell that he really knew how to teach — just like a professor. And, in a certain kind of way he was a professor. What he taught us was how to win. And he did it without ever mentioning winning."

— Dave Meyers, UCLA 1973-75, who played on two national championship teams.

"Coach Wooden is the 'winningest' coach I have ever known in the profession. The way he took great players and molded them into national champions with a sprinkling of overachievers is spectacular."

— Bobby Bowden, former Florida State University football coach

"John Wooden is the greatest coach ever in any sport."

— South Carolina football coach Steve Spurrier

"I think we all overuse the word 'great.' But other than my father, he is the greatest person I've ever met. To have rubbed shoulders with his greatness for 10 years was truly extraordinary."

— Legendary broadcaster Dick Enberg, who was the "voice" of the Bruins 1967-75. ●

Kareem Abdul-Jabbar assists coach John Wooden onto to the court as UCLA celebrated the 40th anniversary of the 1967 NCAA Championship team in 2007.

Wooden, center on bench, puts his hand to his head as his team misses a play in the Pacific Coast Conference championship playoff game with Oregon State College in Corvallis, Oregon on March 4, 1955.

John Wooden's All-Time UCLA Bruins

The following are the young men who played – or were team managers – for UCLA under John Wooden from 1948-49 through 1974-75.

Ackerman, Dick	Boulding, Wayne	Daggott, Andy	Goodrich, Gail
Adams, Carroll	Bragg, Don	Darrow, Chuck	Goss, Fred
Adler, Frank	Brandon, Cliff	Davidson, Jack	Gower, Larry
Alba, Ray	Brewer, Jim	Dexter, Dennis	Graham, Kent
Alcindor, Lewis	Brewer, Lathon	Dishong, Roger	Grandi, Don
Alio, Mike	Bridges, Lloyd	Dodwell, Dave	Grandi, Tim
Allen, Lucius	Brogan, Alan	Donagho, Chuck	Grates, Tom
Alper, Art	Brucker, Steve	Drollinger, Ralph	Gray, Fred
Amstutz, Harlan	Bryant, Bill		Green, John
Anderson, Stan	Buccola, Guy	Eberhard, Gil	Griffith, Neil
Anderson, Tom	Burke, Conrad	Eblen, Bill	Gruber, Edwin
Aranoff, Steve		Ecker, John	Gugat, Rich
Archer, Robert	Camarillo, Al	Elerding, Steve	
Armstrong, Douglas	Carmock, John	Ellis, Bill	Hall, Dave
Arnold, Jack	Carson, Vince	Elzer, Richard	Haisten, Jim
	Caviezel, Jim	Erby, Al	Hansen, Dick
Babcock, Henry	Chambers, Brice	Erickson, Keith	Harrison, Jim
Bailey, Allen	Chapman, Jon	Evans, Jerry	Hazzard, Walt
Baker, Gary	Chasen, Barry		Heitz, Ken
Baker, Jim	Chrisman, Joe	Farmer, George	Helman, Jay
Ballard, Bob	Cline, Neal	Farmer, Larry	Henry, Ted
Ballinger, John	Clustka, Charles	Fields, Richard	Herring, Alan
Bane, Ron	Coleman, Don	Fisher, Robert	Hibler, Mike
Banton, Dick	Conkey, Jim	Franklin, Gary	Hicks, Bill
Barnes, Duane	Conwell, Alan	Frear, Robert	Hill, Andy
Barnett, Greg	Cook, Bruce	Freeman, Wayne	Hirsch, Jack
Bauer, Ralph	Cook, Ray	French, Billy	Hobbs, Doug
Bell, Robert	Corliss, Casey	Friedman, Jerry	Hockins, Lee
Bennett, Eldon	Costello, Mark	Friedman, Lenny	Hoffman, Vaughn
Benoit, Robert	Cox, Bill	Friedman, Les	Hollyfield, Larry
Berberich, John	Crabtree, Fred	Frost, James	Holzer, Fred
Berry, Robert	Crawford, Harold		Huggins, Mike
Betchley, Rick	Crawford, Russell	Galbraith, John	Humphrey, Keith
Bibby, Henry	Crowe, Sam	Gelber, Art	Hurry, Jim
Blackman, Pete	Crum, Denny	Glucksman, Richard	Hutchins, Art
Bond, Ernie	Cumberland, Dave	Glucksman, William	
Bond, Howard	Cunningham, Gary	Goldman, Marvin	Irmas, Dick
Booker, Kenny	Curtis, Tommy	Golnick, Clair	
Boone, Bill		Goodman, Larry	Jacobs, Ron
Borio, Courtney		Goodman, Marvin	Jennings, James

Appendix

Jaeckel, Ralph
Johnson, Don
Johnson, Ernie
Johnson, Marques
Johnson, Nolan
Johnson, Rafer
Johnston, Wm
Jones, Scott
Jones, Warnell
Judd, Randy

Katilius, Vytas
Katz, Dave
Ken, Lindy
Kennedy, Kenfield
Killgore, Dick
Kilmer, Billy
Klein, Phil
Kligman, Eward
Knapp, Don
Kniff, Brian
Kordick, Jack
Kraushaar, Carl
Kropf, Ken
Krupnick, Sid
Kurtovich, Bob

Lacey, Edgar
Land, Don
Lawson, Ron
Lee, Chris
Lee, Greg
Leeds, Art
Leigh, Barry
Levin, Rich
Lewinter, Jeff
Lincoln, Jim
Livingston, Ron
Lock, Steve
Logan, Gene
Long, Bob
Luchsinger, Grover
Lundy, Al
Lynn, Mike
Lynn, Richard
Lyons, John

Marcuccin, Bob
Matlin, Jack
Matney, Ken
Matulich, John
McCarter, Andre
McCollister, Larry
McFarland, Jim
McFerson, Henry
McFerson, Jim

McIntosh, Doug
Meerson, Steve
Meyers, David
Mielke, David
Milhorn, Jim
Miller, Denny
Miller, Kent
Miller, Rene
Miller, Robert
Mills, William
Minishian, Dennis
Mokree, George
Montgomery, James
Moore, Jerry
Moore, John
Moore, Robert
Morgan, George
Morrison, Roger
Mueller, Jim
Mullen, Denny

Nagler, Larry
Nater, Swen
Naulls, Willie
Nesbitt, Fred
Newcomb, John
Newell, Lee
Nichols, Roger
Nichols, Ron
Nielsen, Jim
Nielsen, William
Norman, Jerry

Oldenberg, Neil
Olinde, Wilbert

Parrett, Chuck
Patterson, Steve
Pavlovich, Barry
Pearson, Ron
Perry, Phil
Peterson, Neal
Pollock, Ken
Porter, Barry
Pounds, Robert
Profit, Mel
Pulvers, Tracy
Purdy, Doug
Putnam, Jack

Ramsey, Bob
Ratcliff, Tony
Raymond, Dick
Reigleman, Keith
Reser, Jim
Ridgeway, Dick

Riffey, Jerry
Rippens, Barry
Roane, Mike
Roberds, Dick
Robideaux, Gene
Robinson, Wes
Rogers, Ben
Rojas, Carl
Rosvall, Jim
Rowe, Curtis
Rubino, Ken

Saffer, Don
Saner, Neville
Sapp, Tom
Saunders, Paul
Sawyer, Alan
Schiff, Al
Schofield, Terry
Schultz, Randy
Schwartz, Rick
Siebert, Bill
Seidel, Don
Serafin, Mike
Shackelford, Lynn
Shapiro, Marty
Sheldrake, Eddie
Simmons, Bob
Simon, Robert
Skaer, Dick
Skjervheim, Sonny
Slaughter, Fred
Smith, Bert
Smith, Gavin
Smith, Michael
Snell, Wayne
Spillane, Jim
Stanich, George
Steffanoff, Wayne
Steffen, Jim
Steinman, Henry
Stewart, Kim
Sutherland, Gene
Sutton, Roy
Sweek, Bill

Taft, Morris
Tahti, Nels
Taylor, Kent
Thomas, Andy
Thomas, Marvin
Thompson, Denny
Thompson, Dick
Todd, Roger
Torrence, Walt
Townsend, Raymond

Treat, Ben
Trgovich, Pete

Underhill, Roland
Ureda, Bill

Vallely, John
Van Atta, John
Vana, Daird
Vitatoe, Marvin
Von Hagen, Ron
Vroman, Brett

Wahl, Steve
Walczuk, Lee
Wallace, Ron
Walls, Gary
Walton, Bill
Warren, Mike
Washington, Kenny
Washington, Richard
Waxman, Dave
Wayne, Joe
Webb, Robert
Webster, Larry
Wells, Curtis
Werft, Ron
Wershow, Art
Whitcomb, Ken
White, Eddie
Whitley, Ralph
Wicks, Sidney
Wilkes, Keith
Williams, Dave
Williams, Gene
Williams, Tom
Wills, Bob
Winkelholz, Bill
Winkler, Bill
Winterburn, Ron
Wolf, Mervyn
Wooley, Jim
Wright, Mark

Zelman, Steve
Zullinger, Jack

11·12

TEXACO

| KANSAS | 20 25 45 42 33 | FLS 12 |
| UCLA | 64 34 52 24 25 | 11 |

KANSAS
UCLA

University of Kansas basketball coach Ted Owens and Wooden walk from the Astrodome after UCLA defeated Kansas 68-60 in the NCAA championship semifinal in Houston, Texas on March 25, 1971.